THE IMAGE OF THE OTHER AS ENEMY

THE IMAGE OF THE OTHER AS ENEMY

RADICAL DISCOURSE IN INDONESIA

Muhammad Iqbal Ahnaf

ASIAN MUSLIM ACTION NETWORK

Silkworm Books

This publication is partially funded by The Rockefeller Foundation.

ISBN–10: 974-93619-9-7
ISBN–13: 978-974-93619-9-3

First published in 2006 by
Silkworm Books
104/5 M. 7, T. Suthep, Chaing Mai 50200, Thailand
P.O.Box 296 Phrasingh Post Office, Chiang Mai 50000
E-mail: info@silkwormbooks.com
www.silkwormbooks.com

Original cover photo of Mt. Merapi by Toto Santiko Budi/JiwaFoto
Cover illustration by Silkworm Books. Some images downloaded from internet sources. If copyright holders identify their work we will reimburse them for user fees at Thai market value.

Typeset by Silk Type in Warnock Pro 10 pt.

CONTENTS

FOREWORD

Problematizing views from within "Islam(s)" in Southeast Asia

In 1953 the late Gustav von Grunebaum organized a conference of leading European scholars of Islam, the first to undertake a historical and critical self-understanding of "Islamic studies." The conference examined relationships among Muslims, and between Islam and various cultures. It found that the assumptions and methods used in fields of study like Islamic history lagged a century behind those used in European history. One year later Bernard Lewis remarked that the history of the Arabs had been written primarily in Europe by historians with no knowledge of Arabic and Arabists with no knowledge of history.[1]

Half a century later, research on the subject has changed. There is an increasing number of studies on Islam written by Muslims who know the faith, the cultures, and the practices in different contexts—the works by Akbar Ahmad, Mahmoud Mumdani, Chandra Muzaffar, and Nurcholish Madjid are just a few examples among many. Also changed is the global context itself. Now perhaps more than ever, "Islam" is more than just a description of a fifteen-century-old faith shared by one-and-a-half billion people. The word has strong emotive qualities for those both within and outside the faith. Two decades ago the late Edward Said wrote, "For the right, Islam represents barbarism; for the left, medieval theocracy; for the center, a kind of distasteful exoticism. In all camps, however, there is agreement that even though little enough is known about the Islamic world there is not much to be approved of there."[2] It is therefore important to understand, from their own perspectives, the contemporary problems that Muslims are facing.

Works in this series, Islam in Southeast Asia: Views from Within, join many other writings on Islam by authors at the periphery of scholarship, using assumptions and methods that may no longer differ from those used in the centers of learning. But if such is the case, how is this series different from the other writings on Islam that are presently flooding the popular and academic landscapes?

To state the obvious, this series addresses Islam in Southeast Asia. In relation to the Islamic world, where the sacred geography, history, and language of the Middle East seems to have established that region as the center, Southeast Asia is clearly seen as the periphery. But it is misleading to conceptualize Southeast Asia as a single sociocultural entity. As is true elsewhere in the world, societies in Southeast Asia are heterogeneous. Muslims in Indonesia and Malaysia, for example, lead lives that differ from those in Thailand and the Philippines because of the different realities facing majority and minority populations in the respective countries. Furthermore, whether Muslims constitute a minority or a majority, their lives differ again when seen in contexts influenced by Javanese culture, British colonialism, Filipino Catholicism, or Theravada Buddhism, among other things. In short, the cultural topography of Southeast Asia is a rich multiplicity.

Consequently, Islam as believed in and practiced by people in the diverse worlds of Southeast Asia is not necessarily singular, since there could be as many Islams as the various contexts that constitute them.[3] The problems facing Muslims in Southeast Asia will therefore vary. Those portrayed by researchers in this series are unusual, and their analysis is at times groundbreaking, but what they underscore is that Southeast Asian Muslims struggle with multiple identities in sociocultural contexts destabilized by globalizing forces. In addition, the fact that this research is carried out by young Muslim scholars is important; the "new generation" factor could explain both the distinctive set of problems these researchers are interested in and the fresh approaches they use.

The "views from within" approach, however, is not without its own potential problems. To engage in studies claiming to be "views from within" is in some ways to guard against the study of "others" as the study of one's own self, because in such a situation writers face other types of realities that are possibly distorted in some other ways. It is therefore important for readers to appreciate the effort researchers make to situate themselves at a distance that gives them a better perspective on the social realities of their subject while retaining their sensitivity towards, and ability to relate to, the people they are studying.[4]

At a time when Islamophobia is on the rise,[5] it is essential to find fresh perspectives that will allow us to understand the new problems and tensions facing Muslims in contemporary Southeast Asian societies, and to articulate the ways in which they negotiate their lives as members of communities of faith in a fast-changing world. This series of studies by young Muslim scholars of Southeast Asia is an important step in this direction.

Chaiwat Satha-Anand
Faculty of Political Science
Thammasat University, Bangkok

Notes

1. Azim Nanji, ed., *Mapping Islamic Studies: Genealogy, Continuity and Change* (Berlin and New York: Mouton de Gruyter, 1997), xii.

2. Edward Said, *Covering Islam* (New York: Pantheon, 1981), xv.

3. Aziz Al-Azmeh, *Islams and Modernities* (London and New York: Verso, 1996).

4. I have discussed the problem of alterity in conducting research on Muslim studies in Chaiwat Satha-Anand, *The Life to this World: Negotiated Muslim Lives in Thai Society* (Singapore and New York: Marshall Cavendish, 2005), 25–26.

5. Akbar S. Ahmad, *Islam under Siege: Living Dangerously in a Post-Honor World* (Cambridge: Polity Press, 2004), 36–39.

INTRODUCTION

Islamic fundamentalism, after having been suppressed for three decades by the Suharto regime, is enjoying a wave of resurgence in the increased openness and freedom of Indonesia's post-New Order political climate. Demands for implementing Islamic law or establishing an Islamic state in Indonesia are becoming louder and more vociferous on the part of new Islamic political parties as well as fundamentalist groups. Among the new parties are the Justice Party (PK), Star Crescent Party (PBB), Muslim People's Party (PUI), and United Development Party (PPP); the fundamentalist groups include the Defense Front of Islam (FPI), Majelis Mujahidin Indonesia (MMI), Hizbut Tahrir Indonesia (HTI), Youth Islamic Movement (GPI), and Surakarta Defense of Islam Front (FPIS).[1]

Although the majority of Indonesians are Muslim, the latest survey conducted by Syarif Hidayatullah Islamic State University demonstrated that the country's two largest Muslim organizations, Nahdatul Ulama (NU) and Muhammadiyah, do not support the radicals' agendas. Yet Islamic fundamentalism, especially the proposal to implement Islamic law, is attracting a following as an alternative means of solving social problems, at least in part, because of Indonesia's long-unresolved multidimensional crisis. Moreover, the fundamentalist groups' well-developed organization and flourishing publication programs are evidence of the movement's potential for further growth. Their regular, intensive academic and religious forums and publications are reaching a wide audience throughout Indonesia.

Islamic fundamentalism can be defined as a radical, totalitarian clinging to the belief that the complete establishment of Islamic law is the only way to order the world. Nasr Hamid Abu Zaid, a leading Egyptian Muslim scholar, describes it as "a *weltanschauung* or worldview that seeks to establish its own order, and thus to separate the [Muslim] people from the rest of humanity." (as quoted in Tibi 1998, xi).

The radical and exclusive character of this perspective, which many Indonesians find disturbing, leads the fundamentalists to place themselves and Islam in an antagonistic position toward "the Other"—variously identified as non-Muslims, *kafir*, or infidels. Former Laskar Jihad lawyer Eko Prasetyo, now an activist for a Yogyakarta socialist NGO, personally experienced the intensity of this attitude in his relationships with Laskar Jihad and Majelis Mujahidin Indonesia activists. He views Islamic fundamentalism as a "consciousness of symmetrical opposition between Islam and the West, Islam and Zionism, and Islam and the Christians" (Prasetyo 2002, 275).

One of Islamic fundamentalism's prime characteristics, according to Farid Esack, a liberal South African Muslim scholar, is "enmity towards all who reject fundamentalist views as people who have chosen Evil against God" (Esack 1997, xi). In the same vein, William Liddle, an Indonesia scholar at Ohio State University, talks about the enmity mentality of Islamic fundamentalism, or what he calls Islamic scripturalism. This mentality, according to Liddle, consists of three mindsets: a narrow one that creates a binary opposition between "us" and "them"; a defensive one that views the outside world as the enemy; and a conspiratorial one that sees the outside world as a group efficiently organized to fight Muslims under the leadership of the Jews (Liddle 1998). These studies provide important perspectives on fundamentalism. However, since the image of enemy is not their prime focus, their analyses are derived logically, but somewhat superficially, from the fundamentalists' totalitarian and exclusive paradigm.

The present study delves deeper by examining the actual words and images created by fundamentalists in their publications, speeches, and activities. It addresses the enmity mentality of two fundamentalist Muslim groups, Majelis Mujahidin Indonesia (MMI) and Hizbut Tahrir Indonesia (HTI), by endeavoring to understand the "anatomy" of this attitude. The questions that form the focus of this research are: 1) How are theological roots and historical rationalizations used to create the image of the enemy? 2) How is the image of the enemy developed? 3) How is enmity expressed in actions? And, finally a question for critical analysis: 4) What are the alternatives? What are the possibilities of tolerance within Muslims' perceptions of the Other?

My choice of Majelis Mujahidin Indonesia (MMI) and Hizbut Tahrir Indonesia (HTI) as research subjects is based primarily on an examination of their resources, which demonstrate an intense antagonism toward the Other. Additionally, because these two groups are well organized and have published on these topics, resources are easy to obtain. Moreover, compared with other fundamentalist organizations in Indonesia, MMI and HTI have shown a more ambitious agenda of promoting the implementation of Islamic law through regular publications and intensive programs. MMI has even gone so far as to publish a draft of an alternative Indonesian constitution and penal codes based on Islamic law, which it has proposed to the Indonesian parliament and president.

The promotion of Islamic law has not been the priority of other fundamentalist groups, such as the now disbanded Laskar Jihad and Jema'ah al-Turath al-Islamy, both of which fit under the umbrella of Salafist organizations (revivalist puritan organizations); neither has Islamic law been advocated by organizations like the Islamic Youth Defense or Islamic Youth Defense Surakarta. The Salafists, instead, focus on the purification of Muslims' faith (*'aqidah*) through promoting righteousness and eradicating the sins that lead to polytheism (*shirk*). The objective of both the Islamic Youth Defense and Islamic Youth Defense Surakarta is to glorify the name of Allah by developing an Islamic brotherhood (*ukhuwah Islamiyah*). Their activities include mobilizing solidarity against the persecution of Muslims around the world as well as waging war on gambling dens, brothels, and night spots. Thus, these groups fall outside the scope of this study.

The present research combines field and documentary research methods with a qualitative approach. The field research component is based on data gathered through participatory observation, interviews, and focused group discussions (FGD). It also uses primary data from interviews with prominent Majelis Mujahidin Indonesia and Hizbut Tahrir Indonesia figures, as well as from their speeches and sermons. The documentary research component gathers data from the groups' publications, including books, journals, leaflets, brochures, and materials on their websites, http://www.al-islam.or.id and http://www.majelis.mujahidin.or.id. MMI and HTI have their own publishers, including Wihdah Press (MMI), the Department of Data and Information of MMI, Pustaka Thariqul Izzah (HTI), Wahyu Press (HTI), Al-Izzah Press (HTI), the journal *Al-Wa'ie* (HTI), the journal bulletin *Al-Islam* (HTI), and others. In addition, they use various publications relevant to their ideas, such as *Sabili* and *Suara Hidayatullah*, as well as books, archives, and research materials. The present study analyzes this material, supported by secondary data gathered from books and research reports, after considering background information and profiles of MMI and HTI.

Majelis Mujahidin Indonesia (MMI)

MMI is in fact a young organization. It was established August 5–7, 2000, in Yogyakarta following the first Mujahidin congress, which drew more than a thousand Indonesian Muslim activists and several delegations from foreign countries. Despite its youth, it appears to have already spread throughout the country, with branches in nine provinces, including North and South Sumatra, Jakarta, Yogyakarta, East and West Java, Bali, and East and West Nusa Tenggara.[2]

MMI activists are committed to struggle for the application or formalization of Islamic law (*tathbiq al-shari'ah*) in Indonesia.[3] Key figures are Abu Bakar Ba'asyir, the suspected spiritual leader of Jema'ah Islamiyah, who was chosen twice as *amir* (head) of Ahl al-Hal wal 'Ahd (the group's supreme council or legislative board) and Irfan S. Awwas, who heads the executive board. Ba'asyir confronts his followers with a stark alternative: "we have two choices—life in a nation based upon the Qur'an and Sunnah, or death while striving to implement Islamic law" (Erickson 2000). The historical relationship between Ba'asyir and an earlier Indonesian Islamic movement, Darul Islam (DI), during the period 1948–1962 suggests that MMI's ideology is the continuation of, or at least inspired by DI. Ba'asyir is a veteran of this Kartosuwiryo-led organization, which used armed force in an attempt to establish an Islamic state first in West Java and later in West Sulawesi.[4]

MMI's objective in implementing Islamic law seems to be the more pragmatic form of DI's vision of establishing an Islamic state. DI's failure in this effort led the group to consider a more accommodative and peaceful strategy by which they arrived at the principle that implementing Islamic law does not necessarily require the pre-existence of an Islamic state. In the 2000 Mujahidin congress, which gave birth to MMI, an Islamic state was defined as one that implements Islamic law in its entirety. This definition provides MMI with a diplomatic argument that can circumvent accusations of treason (*makar*). MMI's members argue that their goal is not to establish an Islamic state, but rather, to implement Islamic law; Muslims as Indonesian citizens, they contend, are the majority and have the right to practice their religion as stated in the Indonesian constitution (chapter 29). They do not advocate an "Indonesian Islamic State" or a "United Islamic States of Indonesia," but instead, a "Republic of Indonesia" that implements Islamic law. This less extreme and more accommodative strategy is also apparent in their acceptance of certain democratic elements, particularly the idea of a tripartite governmental system comprised of executive, legislative, and judicial branches, even though they condemn democracy as a non-Islamic (*kufr*) system.[5]

But implementing Islamic law does appear to be a stepping stone toward establishing an Islamic state. MMI's draft of an alternative Indonesian national constitution and penal laws based on Islamic law governs all legal matters, and it demands that the Indonesian constitution be changed to conform to Islamic law. The draft also includes discriminatory provisions, such as the requirement that only a Muslim can be president, and a provision calling for the death sentence for Muslims who convert to other religions. It even suggests that non-Muslims should embrace Islam, and recommends the use of Ahl al-Hal wal 'Ahd as a political system (see MMI's *Usulan Undang-Undang Hukum Pidana*). These stipulations strongly suggest a paradox between MMI's acceptance of democratic elements

5

and its rejection of a non-Islamic system. Implementing Islamic law in all aspects of life would, in fact, amount to establishing an Islamic state under the name of the Republic of Indonesia.

Hizbut Tahrir Indonesia (HTI)

Hizbut Tahrir Indonesia, literally meaning "Liberation Party of Indonesia," is part of an international organization, Hizbut Tahrir, founded in Jerusalem in 1953 by a Palestinian scholar, Taqiyuddin An-Nabhani. Initially it was based primarily in Jordan and Lebanon. Exactly when it began in Indonesia is not clear; however, its ideology first appeared in 1972, when An-Nabhani visited Indonesia.

HTI aims to release Muslims from the degrading position they occupy in the world, which it characterizes as *dar al-kufr* (abode of infidels). At the same time it propagates Islam as the basis of world order by reestablishing the past glory of the Islamic caliphate, described as the abode of Islam, or *dar al-Islam* (Yunanto et al. 2003, 53). In accordance with these objectives, HTI insists that its activities are political and refuses to be identified as a spiritual, scientific, academic, or social organization (Hizbut Tahrir 1999a, 16).

HTI has no organizational structure, central figures, or top leader, in contrast to MMI, which has a strong, nationwide organizational network. Ismail Yusanto, who acts as HTI's spokesman, is the only person who is visible as its representative. Nevertheless, HTI cells can be found in almost every region of Indonesia with the same regular and well-attended activities. For example, in Yogyakarta HTI holds open-group discussions every Sunday in several mosques throughout the city. It has been intensively organizing academic activities to promote a sense of urgency in establishing Islamic law and an Islamic caliphate. Its activities include public sermons, seminars, book discussions, and weekly group dialogues. It also publishes massive numbers of books, weekly bulletins, and monthly journals, and it maintains a website with links to similar websites. For many people these activities demonstrate that HTI is an academic and nonviolent organization. In this way, it has succeeded in obscuring its radical ideology, the most notable aspect of which is to establish an international Islamic caliphate. Unlike MMI, which still sees the possibility of applying Islamic law without becoming an Islamic state, HTI regards establishing an Islamic caliphate as the only way to apply Islamic law. Although HTI identifies itself as a political party, it does not participate in the national elections or any other aspect of the secular system. HTI activists believe that Islamic laws, especially those related to the public, such as *hudud* (law of limitations), *jinayat* (criminal law), and *ta'zir* (penal law), can be administered only by a caliph, and not by individuals, groups, a president, or a prime minister, as in a secular system (Hizbut Tahrir 1999a, 4).

For HTI, the application of Islamic law in a secular state is both problematic and useless. Its members compare it to constructing a mosque on the foundation of a movie theater or nightclub—symbols of *ma'shiat* (decadence). Such a system, they contend, would subsequently lead to compromise, which distorts and amputates parts of Islamic law and places crucial issues like the economy and politics under a non-Islamic system. HTI cites Malaysia and Sudan as examples of the failure of the application of Islamic law in secular states. Although the Islamic Party of Malaysia (PAS) was victorious in the most recent elections in Kelantan and succeeded in applying Islamic law in that state, it failed in a larger sense because the laws of *hudud* (limitations) and *qishash* (mutual laws) are not recognized by Malaysia's federal government (Hizbut Tahrir 2001d, 7). Similarly, in Sudan, the application of Islamic law is incomplete for it is not applied in the southern region, which is inhabited mainly by Christians and animists. This situation forced the Sudanese parliament to make compromises in its legal system, and consequently hundreds of laws in Sudan's 1998 national constitution contradict Islam.

From the viewpoint of HTI, the attempt by Islamic parties to apply Islamic law in secular states has failed in countries that use a democratic

7

system. In Indonesia, Islamic parties were defeated by nationalistic parties; in Malaysia, PAS was defeated by the United Malay National Organization (UMNO); in Jordan, the Ikhwan Party and Islamic Action Front Party lost; and in Egypt, Ikhwanul Muslimun, led by Hassan al-Banna, failed to place its candidates in parliament in 1945.

While several Islamic parties have won, including the Refah Party in Turkey and the Islamic Salvation Front (FIS) in Algeria, their victories were later annulled by secular regimes. (Iskandar 2002, 8–9). Consequently, HTI is striving to uproot the secular system by taking power and establishing an international Islamic caliphate (Hizbut Tahrir 1999a, 31).

Despite their differences, MMI and HTI share the same vision of establishing Islamic law completely in order to liberate people, particularly Muslims, from the modern-day condition that Sayyid Qutb has termed the "sick society" (*jahiliyah*). For MMI, the application of Islamic law is the realization of Muslims' complete devotion to Allah. The duty of humans is *ibadah*, prayer to God (Qur'an 51: 56); Ba'asyir, quoting Ibn Taimiyah, defines it as obedience to all that Allah commands and avoidance of all that Allah forbids, which amounts to applying Islamic law in its entirety (*kaafah*).

MMI proponents believe that the nation will soon be destroyed if it does not enact a complete system of Islamic law. Referring to the Qur'an (17: 70 and 95: 4–6), MMI members believe that humans, as God's best creation, should believe in Allah and do good things following God's order (*amanah*) to govern the world with His rules. If this does not come to pass, humans will degenerate to a state lower than that of animals (Ba'asyir 2003, 2–3). Ba'asyir claims that negligence in applying Islamic law has provoked Allah's anger. He is convinced that Indonesia's national crisis is a form of God's punishment (*adzab*) resulting from laxity in applying God's rules. The Qur'an states:

> Allah doth know those of you who slip away under shelter of some excuse; then let those beware who withstand the Messenger's order, lest some trial befall them, or grievous Penalty be inflicted on them (Qur'an 24: 63).

And fear tumult or oppression, which affected not in particular [only] those of you who do wrong; and know that Allah is strict in punishment (Qur'an 18: 25) (as cited in Al-Anshari 2002, 72).

Regarding the current situation, MMI describes Muslims in Indonesia as a *dhimmi* (protected) majority, whose right to apply Islamic law has been repressed by the non-Muslim minority (Ba'asyir 2003, 5). MMI claims that the Indonesian parliament's refusal to enact the Jakarta Charter of 1945, which obliges Muslims to implement Islamic law in the national constitution, is a kind of forced/collective apostasy (Ba'asyir 2003, 5).

For HTI the application of Islamic law is the manifestation of faith and the realization of the obligation to choose a caliph (Ramadlan 2002, 12). Further, HTI insists that the absence of Islamic law and Muslim authority makes it mandatory for Muslims to declare war on their ruler. HTI proponents are concerned about Muslims' situation worldwide, which they describe as a state of two-fold adversity: divided into disparate nations and governed by infidel countries as the result of the destruction of the Islamic caliphate. Therefore, for HTI, enforcing Islamic law in all aspects of life is the way to liberate Muslims from this adverse situation (Hizbut Tahrir 1999a, 13–14). That is what is meant by being a Muslim, as stated in the Qur'an (5: 49):

And this [His command]: judge thou between them by what Allah hath revealed, and follow not their vain desires, but beware of them lest they beguile thee from any of that [teaching] which Allah hath sent down to thee. And if they turn away, be assured that for some of their crimes it is Allah's purpose to punish them. And truly most men are rebellious (Hizbut Tahrir 1999a, 11).

Because of this shared vision, MMI and HTI are in close alliance. They communicate regularly and participate in each other's programs. Although HTI insists on the need to establish an Islamic caliphate, its main agenda is maintaining the current pressure to apply Islamic law. HTI even actively raises the issue of Islamic law rather than creating an Islamic caliphate. Recently its activists led a demonstration together with other Muslim groups under the banner *"Selamatkan Indonesia Dengan Syari'ah!"* (Save Indonesia with Islamic law!) Prior to the 2004 general election, HTI encouraged Muslims to vote only for those Islamic parties committed to establishing Islamic law.

THE IMAGE OF THE OTHER AS ENEMY

Constructing the Image

On September 10, 2003, more than five thousand people, sweltering in the heat of the sun, filled the fields surrounding Surakarta's main sports stadium. The majority were MMI activists along with a few observers and journalists, both local and foreign. Despite the huge number of people, there was a surprising absence of police, except for intelligence officers, who usually guard large public events in Indonesia. Instead, there were hundreds of teenagers and young adults dressed in military uniforms with turbans and other Muslim prayer head coverings, sticks in hand, and emblems embossed on their shirts explaining each person's division within Laskar Mujahidin. The occasion was a public gathering organized by MMI to open its three-day congress. Almost every five minutes the crowd would shout *takbir*, *"Allah Akbar!"* especially when a speaker ascended the stage to deliver his speech.[6] Several leaders, including HTI spokesman Ismail Yusanto, sat in line onstage waiting their turn to speak. The speeches generally concerned the struggle for Islamic law, criticisms of the West, and the disgraceful situation of Muslims around the world—all aimed at inflaming the crowd's spirit of *dakwah* (the struggle to establish an Islamic state or apply Islamic law) and *jihad.*

For Mujahidins (MMI activists), the single important element missing was Abu Bakar Ba'asyir, the Amir Mujahidin or MMI leader. He was in police custody awaiting trial, accused not only of being the leader of Jema'ah Islamiya, but also of involvement in several bombings in Indonesia and conspiring to kill Indonesian President Megawati. In his absence, Irfan S. Awwas, head of MMI's executive board, read a message from him.

The audience responded to the presentations with loud shouts of *takbir* and raised fists, signifying their united spirit and intense enthusiasm, as if they were prepared to die for the MMI cause. One of the preachers, Luthfi Bashari, the head of a *pesantren* (religious school) in Malang, East Java, and currently a member of MMI's Ahl al-Hal wal 'Ahd (supreme council), led the crowd in *takbir* three times, and then began his speech with the greeting, *"al-salam 'alaikum,"* or "peace upon you," specifically to the Muslims in the audience. He followed this greeting with another, *"al-Syamm 'alaikum,"* or "poison to you," specifically directed at the non-Muslim segment of the audience. This expression of enmity affirms a paragraph in Bashari's MMI-published book (Bashari 2002, 13):

> The enemies of Islam, especially the Jews and Christians, will not relent [in their battle against Muslims] if Muslims around the world still exist and practice the "pure" teachings of Islam from al-Qur'an and Hadith.

Bashari, as Awwas admitted in a personal interview, tends to make harsh and radical statements. However, numerous other expressions identifying the Other as enemy are easy to find in the two groups' publications and their leaders' speeches. Their discourses have systematically constructed, either intentionally or not, the image of the Other as enemy by promoting such antagonistic attitudes as anger, hatred, suspicion, resentment, envy, and hostility toward the Other. For fundamentalists, "the Other" refers to all non-Muslims, whom they identify as *kafir*. Bashari defines them as "people outside of Islam, including *ahl al-kitab* (the people of the book, that is, the Jews and Christians) as well as others such as Magians [an ancient religious community at the time of the prophet Muhammad], Hindus, Buddhists, Shintoists, Confucianists, Sikhs, Taoists, pagans of all kinds, and atheists" (Bashari 2002, 11).

In a similar vein, Shiddiq al-Jawi, a Yogyakarta HTI leader, states that *kafir* enmity to Islam parallels the inevitable and intense conflict between truth and falsehood. He argues that all non-Muslims are hostile to Islam and that this enmity is particularly obvious when Muslims are not in power (personal interview, 2000.) The same view is reflected in the idea that "non-Muslim" is a single community (*al-kufr millah wahidah*). For Abu Haris, an HTI activist in Yogyakarta, the Qur'an clearly insists that all non-Muslims are *kafir*, as it states: "Those who reject (Truth), among the People of the Book and among the polytheists, will be in Hellfire, to dwell therein (for aye). They are the worst of creatures" (Qur'an 98: 6).

In some cases the term *kafir* also refers to Muslims, particularly liberal Muslims who oppose the fundamentalists' views and are regarded as barriers to achieving their goals. This idea is reflected, for example, in the fundamentalists' stance that Muslims who do not regard non-Muslims as *kafir* are themselves *kafir*. It specifically rejects the ideas of pluralist Muslims promoting religious equality. Moreover, there are varying levels of intensity of the image of the enemy, depending on which group is being discussed. The strongest and most frequent image is used in referring to Jews and Christians, or to America and the West. But the enemy also includes the Hindus of India, who are identified as persecutors of Muslims. In addition, the fundamentalists classify atheism and communism as *kufr* ideologies and connect them to the persecution of Muslims, for example, in China and Chechnya.

In the pages that follow I will further elaborate the fundamentalists' image of the enemy. After first discussing the roots of this image, I will describe the fundamentalists' discourse patterns in developing this image. Finally, I will address the implications of this image, particularly the praxis of symbolic violence and its incompatibility with efforts to create peaceful coexistence in a pluralistic society.

ANALYZING THE IMAGE OF THE OTHER

Roots of the Image

The fundamentalists' image of the Other as enemy is rooted in two sources: passages from the Qur'an and *hadiths*, and the history of conflicts between Muslims and non-Muslims. Fundamentalists highlight the Qur'an's confrontational passages regarding the Other while ignoring or reinterpreting the conciliatory passages. They then reinforce the image by listing cases of conflict between Muslims and non-Muslims throughout history.

Theologically, the fundamentalists cite passages from the Qur'an and *hadiths* referring to the perpetual conflict between Islam as truth (*al-haq*) and non-Islam as falsehood (*al-batil*). They believe that this conflict can end only when non-Muslims submit to a Muslim ruler under the status of *dhimmi* (protected). This logic leads them to a black-and-white paradigm that divides the world into two opposing halves: the abode of Islam (*dar al-Islam*) and the abode of *kufr* (*dar al-kufr*). They then cite Qur'anic verses to support this tidy division; for example: "those who believe fight in the cause of Allah, and those who reject faith fight in the cause of evil" (Qur'an 4: 76); and "... for the unbelievers are unto you open enemies" (Qur'an 4: 101; cited in Bashari 2002, 10).

The fundamentalists equate the nature of conflict between Islam and non-Islam with the story of Satan's refusal to obey God's command to prostrate himself before Adam (Qur'an 2: 30 ff). According to this story, the devil was arrogant because he was created from fire, which made him feel superior to Adam, who was created from clay; consequently, Satan felt that it was not appropriate to bow to Adam. This arrogance angered God and He punished Satan with eternal damnation, thereby encouraging him to continually tempt humans to go astray. The following passage refers to this incident.

> He said: "because thou hast thrown me out of the way, lo! I will lie in wait
> for them thy straight way; then will I assault them from before them and

behind them, from their right and their left; nor wilt thou find, in most of them, gratitude for thy mercies" (Qur'an 7: 16–17).

The devil's enmity toward Adam, according to the fundamentalists, is connected to God's pronouncement of perpetual enmity between Muslims and infidels (*kafir*), which all of Allah's prophets have experienced. Bashari identifies this enmity as a theological conflict that necessarily leads to a basic confrontation between Muslims, who defend God's interests, and *kafir*, who are God's enemies (*Sabili* 1999, 31).

Moreover, the fundamentalists frequently refer to the feeling of being under siege. They cite Qur'anic discourse about the Other, which is understood as the nature and the reality of *kafir* enmity toward Islam and Muslims. This enmity, according to Dr. Sa'aduddin As-Sayyid Shalih, arises primarily out of non-Muslims' jealousy and resentment of Islam as a universal and superior religion (Shalih 1999, 2–3). Thus, the fundamentalists feel that Islam and Muslims are always under siege by the *kafir* and their systematically organized power. As the Qur'an (Al-Nisa': 101) literally states, they believe that the *kafir* are the real enemy of Muslims. On the nature of this enmity, Ba'asyir emphasizes several Qur'anic passages: "they [non-Muslims] will not fail to corrupt you, they only desire your ruin; rank hatred has already appeared from their mouths, and what their hearts conceal is far worse" (Qur'an 3: 118, as quoted by Ba'asyir n.d.). Specifically regarding the Jews' and Christians' endless enmity toward Muslims, the following two verses are the most frequently cited:

Nor will they cease fighting you until they turn you back from your faith if they can. And if any of you turn back from their faith and die in disbelief, their works will bear no fruit in this life and in the hereafter; they will be companions of the fire and will abide therein (Qur'an 2: 217).

Never will the Jews or the Christians be satisfied with thee unless thou follow their form of religion (Qur'an 2: 120).

Fundamentalists quote a Qur'anic verse (61: 8) describing non-Muslims' endless enmity to Islam as the desire to extinguish God's light. They understand this notion of the *kafirs'* endless enmity toward Islam as reality and cite Qur'anic references to *ahl al-kitab* (people of the book, or the Jews and Christians) and polytheists (*mushrik*), who, they claim, are conspiring against Islam. The Qur'an touches on the Jews' hatred of Muslims (Qur'an 3: 118); the polytheists' conspiracy to attack Islam (Qur'an 8; 30, 86:15; and cooperation between the Jews, Christians, and *munafiq* (hypocrites or people who pretend to be Muslim) to attack Islam, provide funds to obscure God's way from Muslims (Qur'an 8: 36), create divisions within Islam (Qur'an 5: 110; 6: 7; 10: 76; 27: 13; 34: 43; 46: 7; 2: 102), and attempt to arrest, persecute, and plot against Muslims (Qur'an 8: 30). The fundamentalists also cite a *hadith* comparing Muslims to food that is ravished by packs of voracious wolves, a metaphor for the enemy nations surrounding Muslims (*Al-Islam* 144(9)).

Apart from these notions of being under siege, the fundamentalists' enmity toward the Other is related to their goal of establishing an Islamic system. This goal rests on the belief that all who reject their views and who are potential obstacles to establishing an Islamic system are Islam's enemies. They should be fought until an Islamic system is established, when they will be categorized as *kafir dhimmi* (non-Muslims under the protection of Muslim rulers). The concept of *kafir dhimmi* originally applied in situations where the rulers were Muslim. In an Islamic state, non-Muslims are basically divided into two categories, *kafir dhimmi* and *kafir harb*. The former are non-Muslims who submit to Islamic rule. To these people, Islam gives protection; however, they must pay *jizyah*, a special tax. The latter category consists of non-Muslims who refuse to submit to Islamic rule. Islamic law commands that these people be persuaded to accept the status of *kafir dhimmi*; if persuasion fails, Islam commands initiating a holy war against them until they accept Islamic law and pay *jizyah* (Qur'an 9: 29).

In contemporary times, however, in the absence of an Islamic system or Islamic state, fundamentalists view all who reject their desire to establish an Islamic state as the enemy—as people who have chosen evil instead of God and who will remain the enemy until an Islamic state is established and they accept the status of *kafir dhimmi*. Fundamentalists find support for these notions in several passages of the Qur'an. These passages include God's prohibition against taking the Jews and Christians as leaders (Qur'an. 5: 51), God's prohibition against Muslims taking *kafir* as their *wali* (protectors) (Qur'an 3: 28, 4: 144, 159) and close friends (Qur'an 60: 1), a verse that tells of the strong attitudes of Muhammad and his companions towards *kafir* (Qur'an 48: 29), and verses that command Muslims to fight those who reject submission to an Islamic ruler (Qur'an 9: 29, 123, 2: 190, 191; 4: 75; 8: 60).

Anticipating non-Muslims' endless enmity toward Islam, Ba'asyir warns Muslims that the only way to deal with it is by governing non-Muslims under Islamic law. Because he distrusts non-Muslims, he argues that the application of Islamic law is a way to control non-Muslims' attitudes toward Muslims. Although the fundamentalists do admit that the Qur'an allows for the coexistence of Muslims and non-Muslims, their willingness to coexist with non-Muslims is accompanied by a sense of suspicion. For example, Irfan S. Awwas, in commenting on the late Indonesian Christian inter-religious dialogue activist Th. Sumarthana, said, "He is a good man; I respect him, but, unfortunately, he is a Christian, we should be careful" (personal interview).

Fundamentalists cite examples of clashes that have occurred throughout history and the "reality" of *kafirs'* endless enmity to support these theologically based arguments concerning the perpetual conflict between Islam and non-Islam. They believe that these incidents are all connected to each other in the chain of the *kafirs'* global conspiracy against Islam. The following paragraphs from *Al-Wa'ie* 3(1) November 24, 2000, articulate this belief.

> Whatever crisis happened to the Muslim world is related to the wicked conspiracy of the enemies of Islam. Long before the downfall of *khilafah* (Islamic state), they had already made a systematic strategy to destroy

khilafah and clean up its ruins by creating traps to make Muslims lose their Islamicity.

> The crises in Palestine, Lebanon, Bosnia, Kosovo, Chechnya, Eritrea, Chad, Pantai Gading, Somalia, Kashmir, Turkestan, Xianjiang, Moro, the Moluccas and Irian Jaya are evidence of the conspiracy of the enemies of Islam.

Fundamentalists recall the conflicts between Muslims and non-Muslims both in the past and in the present to prove the reality of the image of the enemy as told in the Qur'an. This attempt is seen in another selection from the same *Al-Wa'ie* article.

> All the dignity and honor that Muhammad created for Muslims was soiled by *kafir*. Muslims' blood as a symbol of their dignity and honor was spilled in front of their eyes without any defense. The obvious examples are the Jews' killing of and cruelty toward Muslims in Palestine, the Russian military's killing and cruelty of Muslims in Chechnya, Indian Hindus' killing of and cruelty toward Muslims in Kashmir, and the United States' killing of and cruelty toward Muslims in Afghanistan.

Building on these historical events, the fundamentalists refer to what they call non-Muslims' attacks on Islam, of which there are two kinds—physical and non-physical (ideological) attacks. In discussing physical attacks, fundamentalists tend to repeat stories about conflicts between Muslims and non-Muslims from the past. Examples include the collaboration of the Christians, Jews, and Meccan polytheists in attacking Muslims in Medina, which ended in the battle of Khaibar; cooperation between the Jews and Christians in the Ahzab battle; the Jews' killing of Umar Ibn Khattab; the Jews playing Uthman Ibn Affan against Ali Ibn Abi Talib; Christians' attack on Muslims in the battles of Mut'ah, Tabuk, Yarmuk, and so forth. Other past and current conflicts that they mention are listed below.

The Crusades
They were the realization of Christians' resentment and hatred of Muslims, as they conquered areas where Christians had previously ruled, especially since Umar Ibn Khattab took Bethlehem from the Roman Empire (Amhar 2003, 16–17).

Imperialism
This is the continuation of the Crusades that targeted the Muslim world (Hizbut Tahrir 2003b, 3–4).

Israeli-Palestinian conflict
This is the non-Muslims' way of dividing Muslims by placing the Jews in the heart of the Muslim world in the Middle East. It aims to stop the rise of Islamic states (Purwandana 2002, 5).

The tragedy of Bosnia
This is a continuation of the Crusades, because in this war, the Serbs shouted slogans from the Crusades. The Catholic Serbs, supported by Western Christian countries, ethnically cleansed Bosnian Muslims (Romli 2002, 11).

The Algerian regime's repression of Muslims
The secular regime in Algeria, supported by the u.s. and the French, attempted to stop the realization of an Islamic system in Algeria. The military regime annulled the victory of FIS (Islamic Salvation Front) in 1991. Algeria's military regime repressed the FIS activists. Hizbut Tahrir claims that there were no fewer than 150,000 Muslims killed and more than 10,000 Muslim activists sent to concentration camps in the Sahara Desert; and that mosques and social centers were closed down in this process (Hizbut Tahrir 2002b; *Sabili* 1999, 27–30).

Kafir-Hindus versus Muslims in Kashmir, India
This is an attempt by infidel Hindus in India to impose the Hindu system on Muslim society in Kashmir. During 1947–1948, fundamentalist Hindus

killed thousands of Muslims, forced Muslim women to convert and Muslim men to marry Hindu women to separate them from their children. This is also identified as part of the West's plan to divide and weaken Muslim power in South Asia.[7]

New Order (Order Baru): "Depoliticization" and repression of Indonesian Muslims

The New Order was an anti-Islam power, which repressed political participation of Muslims. The "depoliticization" of Muslims is based on the government's hatred of Islam, in cooperation with the Indonesian military, because of concern that Islam would be a threat after the decline of communism. This attempt was associated with a master plan made by the Center for Strategic Issues Studies (CSIS), an organization formerly connected with Christians led by Ali Mutopo, which saw Islam as "a barrier to the development of the state." This plan was implemented by creating a scenario to discredit and repress Islam. Leaders and members of Muslim activist groups were sent to jail and many of them disappeared or were killed. Cases often referred to in this context are the tragedies of Tanjung Priok; Woyla; DOM (Daerah Operasi Militer, or Military Operations Area, a campaign against rebel activity) in Aceh; Talangsari Lampung; the killing of kiais' in Banyuwangi; Komando Jihad; NII (Negara Islam Indonesia, or Islamic State of Indonesia, a former Islamic rebel movement); Ambon; and the cases of Usrah and Pesantren Kilat (Al-Chaidar and Tim Peduli Tapol International Amnesty 1998, ix).

Persecution of Muslims in Moro, Philippines

The Philippines situation is part of the way that Western imperialism (uslub isti'mar) prevented the rise of Muslim power in Southeast Asia. Muslims in Moro were the victims of the Christian army of the Philippines, where Muslims were killed in the tragedy of Jabila (Abdurrahman 2002, 17).

Karimov regime persecution of Muslims in Uzbekistan

The Karimov regime is "Jewish-kafir." Since 1997, the Karimov regime has used the war on terrorism to attack Muslim activists. Hizbut Tahrir is the object of this attack because of its political goal to establish an Islamic state, *khilafah Islamiyah*. A Hizbut Tahrir leader, Farhad Usmanov, was killed by the Karimov regime and many members of Hizbut Tahrir are being hunted by Karimov (Hizbut Tahrir n.d.j).

Persecution of Muslims in Xianjiang, China
Communist Russia and China repressed and discriminated against Muslims in Xianjiang, giving them no access to education, employment, medical care, etc. Muslim schools and activities in mosques were abandoned, wearing *jilbab* (headcovers) was banned, and Chinese were encouraged to marry Muslims through assimilation programs.

Christian-Muslim conflict in the Moluccas
This is a u.s. scenario to justify the war on terrorism in Indonesia. This scenario is part of Western imperialism in Muslim countries like Indonesia. *Al-Wa'ie* describes the conflict in the Moluccas as "the periodic crusade that began when the Portuguese Christians colonized this island."[8]

American war in Afghanistan
This is part of the u.s. plan to embed its power within the Muslim population in Central Asia to prevent the rise of Muslim power (Hizbut Tahrir 2002c, 4).

War on Terrorism and Iraq
This is the second Crusade. The West's anti-Islamic attitude, led by the United States, shows that after the Crusades they still want revenge against Islam; therefore, the war on terrorism and on Iraq are evidence of that vengeance (Ismail 2003, 9; Hizbut Tahrir n.d.h).

Others
Persecution of Muslims in Chechnya and in Pattani, Thailand; the tragedies in Somalia, Chad, Pantai Gading (Indonesia), Kosovo, Lebanon, Eritrea, Turkestan, and Irian Jaya.

Fundamentalists describe still another category of non-Muslim attacks consisting of what they call *ghazw al-fikr* or *al-siro' al-fikr,* the battle of ideas. This battle is identified as the next strategy of the Crusades. According to Shalih, "Christians, following their loss in the Crusades, prepared new armies with a new face to fight Muslims, armies without guns and missiles, but armies with ink and paper" (Shalih 1999, 40). Fundamentalists believe that these non-physical attacks on Islam are directed at Muslims' faith (*'aqidah*) and ideology (particularly the idea to implement *shariah* or establish an Islamic state), because these two things are the keys to Muslim power.

To attain these goals, non-Muslims, according to the fundamentalists, have created four programs. The first is *tasykik,* or creating doubts and trivializing Islam. This has been done, for example, by degrading the Qur'an, Hadith, and Muhammad, and by creating propaganda claiming that Islamic laws are irrelevant in the contemporary world. The second program is *tasywih,* meaning an attempt to eradicate Muslims' pride in their religion, and is accomplished by creating negative images of Islam. The third is *tadzwih,* which means syncretizing *kafir* ideas and Islamic ideas to create confusion among Muslims regarding their way of life. The fourth is *taghrib,* or Westernizing the Muslim world in order to influence Muslims to accept Western ideas (Romli 2000, 17).

The fundamentalists see these programs imposed on the Muslim world through Christianization, orientalism, secularism, capitalism, democracy, nationalism, human rights, civil society, religious modernism, pluralism, inter-religious dialogue, freedom of belief, feminism, globalization (including the IMF, World Bank, WTO, CGI), Islamic liberalism, 4-S's (Singing, Sex, Sports, and Smoking), 4-F's (Fun, Fashion, Food, and Faith), "Islamic fundamentalism," and terrorism. They even identify world peace and anti-war campaigns as part of anti-Islamic ideas in that they stifle the Muslims' spirit of *jihad* to fight against *kafir* hostilities and struggle for the establishment of Islamic rule.[9]

Discourse Patterns Used in Constructing the Image

In analyzing the discourses discussed above, one can discern four patterns that the fundamentalists use in developing the image of the Other as enemy: 1) ideologization, 2) demonization, 3) insistence on the idea of the "clash of civilizations," and 4) imagining the victory of Islam.

First, ideologization refers to the fundamentalists' tendency to find an anti-Islamic bias when they analyze conflicts, particularly those that involve Muslims and social issues. Fundamentalists stress anti-Islamic goals not only in cases with strong Muslim versus non-Muslim nuances, but also in non-religious conflicts. For example, although many people see that it is too simplistic to attribute the conflicts in Ambon, Poso, Palestine, Chechnya, and Kashmir to religious motives, the fundamentalists view all these conflicts as having an anti-Islamic agenda.

Moreover, although many Muslims in general feel besieged by the U.S. war on terrorism and its attack on Iraq because of the wide-ranging consequences to Muslims around the world, they do not see religion as the only factor. However, for the fundamentalists, these cases are definite proof of *kafir* hatred and enmity. They even identify the U.S. attack on Iraq as a *"Salib-Davidian"* war on Islam.[10]

In addition, the fundamentalists identify anti-Islamic motives in the separatist Aceh Freedom Movement (GAM) and view the conflict as part of Western strategies to divide the Muslim world by separating a region of a Muslim state. They base this conclusion on the involvement of an international organization, the Henry Dunant Center (HDC) in Aceh. They buttress this argument by pointing out that the victims of the Aceh conflict are Muslims (Hizbut Tahrir n.d.m). To give added emphasis to the anti-Islam goals of this conflict, Irfan S. Awwas accused Hasan Tiro, the leader of the Aceh Freedom Movement (GAM) who lives in Sweden, of being a convert to Judaism (personal interview with Awwas).

Another example of ideologization is the fundamentalists' identification of loans from international money-lending institutions (including the IMF, World Bank, and CGI) to parts of the Muslim world as a *kafir* way of controlling Muslim countries (Hizbut Tahrir n.d.f). Still another example is their identification of Pancasila (the five bases of Indonesian nationality) as a product of the Zionist Freemasonry movement against Islam (Thalib and Awwas 1999).

The fundamentalists further ideologize in their analysis of social and economic issues in Indonesia, such as the multidimensional crisis, corruption, collusion, nepotism, floods, droughts, privatization of state companies, separatism, etc. They emphasize the failure of secular systems and attribute these problems to the lack of an Islamic system of law. Anti-Islamism also features in the fundamentalists' creation of discourse of religious conflict, such as Christian armies of the Philippines, *kafir* Americans, Hindu armies in Kashmir, and others.

The second pattern fundamentalists use in developing the image of the Other is demonization. Their methods are both verbal and visual. Fundamentalist discourse describes the Other as demon-like in its barbarous, cruel, uncivilized, and threatening interactions with Muslims. In his recorded preaching, Ba'asyir resorts to creating a theological basis in his demonizing. Quoting a paragraph in the Qur'an (6: 112), he characterizes *kafir* as a visible (human) form of Satan, compared to Jinn as an unseen form. Both kinds of Satan, according to Ba'asyir, battle continuously against Islam; therefore, Muslims should not be close friends, cooperate, or make any agreements with *kafir* (Ba'asyir n.d.).

The fundamentalists' publications demonize the Other in two ways. The first is by illustrating the Other's hostilities toward Muslims through words and visual images, including videos, pictures, and caricatures. This demonization is articulated in repeated stories about non-Muslims' victimizing Muslims in Palestine, Bosnia, Kosovo, Chechnya, Kashmir, Ambon, Poso, etc. America and the Jews are the most frequent objects of demonization. HTI, for instance, made a list of a hundred aggressive American acts that have killed millions of people around the world through military operations. A leaflet published by HTI says, "Cooperation with America: A criminal act that is forbidden (*haram*) in Islam" (http://www.al-islam.or.id/leaflet).

No less hostile, an edition of *Al-Islam* creates a menacing image of Jews with its title, *"Kobarkan Perang Melawan Yahudi!"* (Inflame war against the Jews!). It describes the Jews as people who tend to deceive, break agreements, dissemble, twist words, and have the strongest enmity toward Islam. Another *Al-Wa'ie* article explains certain Qur'anic verses as God's promise that the Jews will be despised (Qur'an 2: 61), destroyed (Qur'an 17: 4–5), and made homeless; it describes them as people who create destruction (Hizbut Tahrir 2000d). An article in *Al-Wa'ie* explains in detail the steps taken by the United States and the Jews to rule the world (Hizbut Tahrir 2000b). When such so-called *kafir* strategies or conspiracies are reported repeatedly in fundamentalist publications, they can create a frightening image of non-Muslims, especially when accompanied by a theological explanation, such as *"senantiasa memusuhb Islam"* (endless enmity to Islam).

Demonization also includes stories about violence committed against the fundamentalist leaders and members, including arrests, assassinations, and discrimination, which are flavored with the idea of non-Muslims' enmity to Islam in order to create hatred and anger toward the Other. *Al-Wa'ie*, for example, contains a special section, entitled *Akhbar Al-Wa'ie* (*Al-Wa'ie* news), that reports the activities of Muslim activists and situations around the world. Examples include accounts on the Russian military's hostility toward Chechnya, the u.s. military's mass killings in Afghanistan, repression of Muslim activists by the Uzbekistan government, CIA torture of Al-Qaedah members, discrimination against Hizbut Tahrir in Germany, the killing of 322 children during the Intifadah in Palestine, and discrimination against and killing of Muslims in Xianjiang, China. Another example is a corner in *Akhbar Al-Wa'ie* that identifies Reuven Koret, publisher of *Israel Insider* and CEO of Koret Communications, as an Israeli-American. It reports that he called for the destruction of Islam, especially the Ka'bah, in his writing, "Time to Target the Ka'bah" (Hizbut Tahrir 2001j).

Another kind of verbal demonology is describing the Other as a dangerous threat to Muslims. It characterizes the Other as evil by cataloging the failure of secular or non-Islamic systems. In R. C. Mitchell's categories of dehumanization, this type of demonology creates a dichotomy between one group as "civilized" and the other as "uncivilized." An edition of *Al-Wa'ei* focuses on Maman Kh's writing on the failure of Western positive law, which he identifies as the product of secularism, especially in the United States. Its failure, he claims, can be seen in the increase of crime, abortion, divorce, the breakdown of the family, pre-marital sex, HIV/AIDS, and homosexuality. To support his argument, Maman quotes statistics from Stanley K. Henshaw and Evelyn Morrow (1990, 22) showing the high rates of divorce and HIV infection in Western countries such as the U.S., Denmark, Sweden, Italy, Norway, and Finland. Maman attributes the failure of positive law to its fighting the law of God (Maman Kh 2001, 7–13).

Demonization also includes such statements as "Democracy is garbage civilization," "Unity in Diversity (*Bhineka Tunggal Eka*) is a barren system and the cause of national disintegration," "America, the real terrorist," "The West is an animal civilization," "Non-Muslim enmity to Islam," "The biggest enemies of Islam," "Conspiracy network against Islam," "The second edition of the Crusades," "America should be fought," and "Inflame war against the Jews."

Creating visual images of the hostilities against Muslims has also become a daily activity for some fundamentalists. HTI leader Shiddiq Al-Jawie, in an interview, displayed pictures on his computer of victimized Muslims in Chechnya, Palestine, and Ambon. His computer contains videos of Muslims in Chechnya who were slaughtered by the Russian army. During 2000–2001, a video on the killing of Muslims in Ambon was shown repeatedly to limited audiences. Videos on Mujahidin in a *jihad* training camp in Chechnya, and the brutality of the Indonesian police as they transferred Abu Bakar Ba'asyir from a hospital in Solo to Jakarta were played constantly during the September 2003 Mujahidin congress in Solo and were sold out.

In addition, the fundamentalists create terrifying caricatures of hostilities against Muslims. A cover of a book published by Wihdah Press, for example, depicts a close-up of two threatening eyes with non-Muslim symbols (a cross, the Star of David, and a swastika) in the pupils. On another book cover the same symbols appear on the head wrap above a man's face looming over a crowd of people. Following are some examples of these images, with the English translations of their captions.

FIG. 1. *"Previously, the roof of a mosque displayed the name of Allah. Now, in many mosques, this has been replaced by the Ambon Cross."*

FIG. 2. *"Graffiti on a wall insulting the holy place of Muslims after the mosque was burned by Obet"* [the term for Christian fighters in Ambon].

FIG. 3. *"In every mosque that is burned down, a cross is always drawn on the wall as an announcement that the place is controlled by Obet."*

FIG. 4. *"This mosque was burned three times, but because of Allah's help, the fire was always extinguished. Finally, the fourth time, the 'cross fighters' destroyed it."*

FIG. 5. *"The holy Qur'an, which was burned by the Christians, la'natullah [may Allah punish them]. May Allah reduce them to ashes like the Qur'an they have burned."*

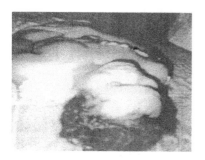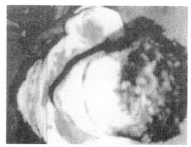

FIGS. 6 AND 7. "Some of the victims of the ruthless kafir, who slaughter humans like animals. This ruthless act occurred on February 23, 1999 in Ambon."

FIG. 8. "Fire at the At-Taqwa mosque; a cross was drawn on its wall. This incident happened on February 23, 1999 in Wailette village."

FIG. 9. *"The barbarians' insult to our Prophet Muhammad; ask the Moluccans the meaning of* cuki *[pig]. There are also many more insults."*

FIG. 10. *"They treated Muslims in Ambon more ruthlessly than the Israeli army did in Palestine; for Obet, Ambon is a small Israel; they carried out Muslim cleansing."*

FIG. 11. (L) The cover of Sa'aduddin As-Sayyid Shalih's book, "Conspiracy Network against Islam." FIG. 12. (R) The cover of Luthfi Bashari's book, "The Big Enemies of Islam: Zionism, Secularism, Atheism, Syncretism, Salibism, JIL (Liberal Islam Network), and Opportunism."

The third discourse pattern is the concept of the inevitable clash of civilizations, particularly between Islam and the rest of the world. The fundamentalists have been good students of Samuel Huntington in his controversial thesis on the "clash of civilizations." Insistence on this issue is articulated in the title of a book published by HTI, *The Inevitability of the Clash of Civilizations (Hamiyyah Siro' al-Hadharah)*. Fundamentalists reduce Huntington's prediction of a future that will be colored by a clash of three civilizations—the West, Confucianism, and Islam—to an inevitable clash between Islam and all other civilizations, especially the West.[11]

This idea is rooted in the fundamentalists' belief in the Islamic system's superiority and comprehensiveness. Implicit in this belief are the notions of inevitable conflict between Islam and non-Islam and the hostile nature of non-Muslims toward Muslims. Fundamentalists divide civilization into two types: spiritually divine and man-made. They define the former as the true civilization, of which Islam is the only example, and Indian and Western civilizations as man-made civilizations, which are false. For them, there is no way to integrate various systems to order the world because civilization, when it is adopted, must be adopted together with the premises upon which it is based. Islamic civilization, the basis of which is revelation, contradicts all non-Islamic civilizations, which are based on the agreement of the people. Even when it appears that there is a kind of meeting of some concepts in Islam and other civilizations, this is not a rational, coherent agreement. Thus, they suspect that the idea of dialogue among civilizations is a non-Muslim scheme to anesthetize Muslims in order to cause them to leave their faith ('aqidah) and their ideological understanding of Islam as a comprehensive system of life (Hizbut Tahrir 2000a, 9).

All the concepts of the dialogue promoting the idea of equality between religions and civilizations, such as mutual acceptance without judgment and seeking commonalities, completely contradict Islam. Fundamentalists argue that those concepts are infidel ideas because the Qur'an makes a clear distinction between Islam and infidels—al-haq (truth) and al-bathil (false-hood)—and always pronounces judgment on what is truth when it mentions the thoughts of infidels. The idea of finding common sense as deduced from the term "kalimatun sawa" is slandering Allah because Allah prohibits any mixing of truth and falsehood (Hizbut Tahrir 2000a, 17–28).

Therefore, a clash between Islamic civilization and other civilizations is real and inevitable. The following quote strongly articulates this idea.

How strange for the one claiming Islam, when he equates Islam with kufr, atheism (ilhad) with trinity and tauhid, the denial of the prophethood of Muhammad with the believers in it, permitting riba and forbidding it, the worship of Allah and worshipping creatures, fornication and marriage, permitting homosexuality and forbidding lesbianism and homosexuality, the pig and dates. It is even more strange; the one who remains silent and says nothing about preference and does not prefer *tawheed* to polytheism, *halal* and *haram*, the Shari'ah to *al-taghut*, the believer to the *kufr*, revelation to man-made, Islam to the remaining *deens*, the Qur'an to the distorted books, worshipping the Creator to worshipping the sun, the cow and the stars. May Allah save us from *fitnah*! Subordination (*tab'iyyah*) is rejected, equality is rejected, and reminding about the preference of Islam and its civilization over the remaining religions and civilizations is rejected (Hizbat Tahrir 2000a, 19).

For the fundamentalists, the clash between Islamic civilization and others is an ideological necessity. It has been occurring since the beginning of Islam, and it will end only when Islam becomes the sole civilization in a new single *ummah*, or society (Hizbut Tahrir 2000a, 34). To support this contention, they constantly list the conflicts between Muslims and non-Muslims throughout history.

The fundamentalists emphasize the inevitability of the clash of Islam and other civilizations by using the moment of the Soviet Union's collapse in 1987, which signified the downfall of communism. They argue that with the downfall of socialism, the American-led global domination of capitalism no longer meets any resistance except from the Islamic world. This is because the rest of the nations in the world have already embraced capitalism. Russia, having renounced communism, is conforming to capitalism. States that claim to be socialist, such as China, North Korea, Vietnam, and Cuba, in reality, are also gradually turning to capitalism. Other states in Latin America, the Far East, and Southeast Asia, and some countries in Africa do not have any ideology that significantly rivals capitalism. Therefore, what the fundamentalists call the "Islamic *ummah*" will be the only nation to wage war on capitalism. Even though the creation of the Islamic *ummah* is not yet complete, as none of the current governments of Muslim countries implement the Islamic system, fundamentalist rhetoric warns Western capitalist countries, especially America, that the power of the Islamic caliphate will be restored to the level it held before it was destroyed (Hizbut Tahrir 1996, 8–9).

The fundamentalists view the current phenomena across the world in this context, especially since the September 11, 2001 tragedy and other cases following it, such as the u.s. attack on Afghanistan and Iraq and the war on terrorism (Sajid 2001a, 10). President George W. Bush's speech after the attack on the World Trade Center and the Pentagon made a strict demarcation of the world: one is either with the United States or with terrorism. According to Ahmad Sajid writing in *Al-Wa'ie*, this speech epitomized the era of the clash between the West and the rest, precisely, between the West and Islam. Sajid concluded his article with the warning: "Now is the time for Muslims to drown Western civilization, which has caused Muslims despair and disaster. Conflict is a logical and necessary consequence" (Sajid 2001a, 17).

The fourth discourse pattern is imagining Islam's imminent victory over the entire world. In Mitchell's theory of conflict, imagining victory fulfills the need to maintain a "positive own-party image"—to think well of oneself and badly of the other. It generates feelings of self-esteem and security through the idea that the group is seen to possess desirable qualities and to behave in a worthy manner (Mitchell 1981, 86–87). Similarly, in Mark Jeurgensmeyer's concept of cosmic war, the eternal war between truth (*al-haq*) and falsehood (*al-batil*) promotes the feeling that one group is on the right side, so that God will defend it, and the others are on the wrong side, so that God will destroy them (Jeurgensmeyer 2000, 140). The imagined victory is based on Qur'anic verses that are understood as God's promise to grant victory.

> God has promised to those among you who believe and work righteous deeds that He will, of a surety, grant them in the land, inheritance [of power], as He granted it to those before them; that He will establish in authority their religion—the one which He has chosen for them; and He will change [their state] after the fear in which they [lived], to one of security and peace (Qur'an 24: 55).

> In the end We deliver Our apostles and those who believe: thus is it fitting on Our part, that We should deliver those who believe! (Qur'an 10: 103).

Fundamentalists find the promise of victory in some of the *hadiths* of Mohammad.

Islam will certainly reach areas which are covered by day and night. Allah will never leave both good and bad houses without bringing His religion into them; honor the honorable and humble the humble. Honor because Allah honors them with Islam and humble because Allah humbles them because of their infidel nature (*kufr*) (*Muwatta Ahmad*).

The end of the day (*qiyamat*) will not come until Muslims fight the Jews, who will hide behind a stone and the stone will say: "Oh Muslims, here is a Jew behind me, come here and kill him (*Sahih Muslim*) (Hizbut Tahrir 2002e).

Fundamentalists believe that the current conditions in which Muslims find themselves—that is, being downtrodden, oppressed, and despised—is a period of transition leading toward the resurgence of Islam. A *hadith* describes this situation as follows: "Islam came in a strange situation, and will be strange again as in the first time. Therefore be happy, people who feel strange."

In certain other fundamentalist publications, imagining a Muslim victory also addresses *qiyamat*, "the story of the end of the day," as told in a *hadith*. It says that Muslims will be the final victors in the war and succeed in destroying the Jewish army as the *hadith* above states. The belief in Islam as the victor is also reflected in the story of the phases of Islamic history that will end with Muslim victory. According to the story, there will be four phases of Islamic history: prophethood, Islamic caliphate, oppressive or dictator kings, and the resurgence of the Islamic caliphate that follows the Prophet's way. The resurgence of the Islamic caliphate will be the end of Muslim history (Tanjung n.d). Following this framework, Fathi Salim refutes Francis Fukuyama's thesis that the domination of capitalism and the collapse of socialism signify the end of history. Instead, he is convinced that the end of history will be the victory of Islam. He argues that Islam is the only civilization that will be dominant; all other civilizations will be destroyed because rather than fulfilling human faith and consciousness, they contradict reason and human nature. He adds that today people are starting to turn away from Western civilization, toward Islamic civilization. This trend, according to Salim, is in accordance with Allah's saying, "God has promised to those among you who believe and work righteous deeds. . ." and with Muhammad's saying, "This preaching will encompass all that night and day encompass" (Salim 2003, 42).

The fundamentalists cite contemporary realities as indications of God's promise of Islam's worldwide victory. The first indication is the collapse of global capitalism as evidenced in the worldwide economic crisis. The crisis of two of the biggest multinational corporations, Enron and WorldCom, according to Tun Kelana Jaya (2002), exposed the vulnerability of the stock exchange and the money market as supporters of the capitalist financial system. Enron's collapse was revealed in the radical drop in its stock value from $1 billion to $0.45 cents, while the collapse of WorldCom was signaled by its failure to fulfill its income target of $1.4 billion a year. The collapse of these huge corporations through financial scandals, as well as that of other multinational corporations, such as Xerox, Arthur Andersen, Global Crossing, Adelphia Communication, Tyco International, ImClone System, and Merc, caused a plummet in values in world stock exchanges. It proved the stock exchange's vulnerability as the supporter of the capitalist financial system.

The money market likewise demonstrated the capitalist financial system's weakness, whereby world capital in developed countries was trapped in non-real sectors, such as stocks, obligations, commercial papers, promissory notes, and so forth. In addition, speculators could easily control the system, causing the rapid movement of large amounts of capital, allowing it to destabilize states' or state companies' stock (Jaya 2002).

The second indicator of Islam's imminent victory, according to fundamentalists, is the failure of three types of Western conspiracy against Islam. First, the West, according to the fundamentalists, failed in its attempt to subvert Islamic thoughts by infiltrating them with foreign ideas, such as secularism, nationalism, democracy, socialism, liberalism, gender equality, pluralism, etc., because of Muslims' commitment to study Islam and the strong movement toward applying Islamic law. Second, the West failed to convince the world that secular civilization is ideal. Muslims view Western civilization as being in a state of collapse, and this view strengthens their belief in the survival of Islamic civilization. Third, the West's imperialistic attempts to co-opt leaders of Muslim countries have instilled hatred among Muslims toward these leaders. This was evidenced in the attitudinal differences between Muslims around the world who opposed the u.s. attack on Afghanistan, while Muslim leaders who gathered in the Organization of Islamic Conference (oic) supported the u.s. attack. Fourth, *kafir* strategy, according to fundamentalists, involves continued military or physical attacks on Islam. This strategy is obvious from u.s. attempts to create military bases in Muslim countries in the Middle East, the Persian Gulf, East Asia, and Southeast Asia, in order to incite conflicts in these regions. The fundamentalists believe that these attempts will fail because Muslims are committed to uphold Islam as their ideology (Hizbut Tahrir 2000c and n.d.d).

The third indicator of Islam's coming victory is the potential of the Muslim world. The fundamentalists, in addition to believing in the superiority of Islamic ideology, mention four features of the Muslim world as potential factors in the victory of Islam. First, geographically, the Muslim world occupies strategic areas in the world's economic routes. Muslim territories include the Straits of Gibraltar in the western Mediterranean, the Suez Canal in the eastern Mediterranean, Gulf Bab al-Mandab (covering small straits in the Red Sea), the Dardanelles and the Bosphorus Straits that form a trade line to the Mediterranean, the Gulf of Hormuz, and the Straits of Malacca. Second, economically, the Muslim world is a rich area containing significant amounts of the world's essential raw materials, including 60 percent of the world's oil reserves, 40 percent of its boron, 50 percent of its phosphate, 60 percent of its perlite, 27 percent of its stronium, and 22 percent of its tin. Third, the total population of Muslims is no less than a billion, i.e. 20 percent of the world's entire population. This large number of Muslims, according to the fundamentalists, can create immense military power. Fundamentalists quote data from the CIA *World Fact Book* enumerating the extraordinary number of military personnel in Muslim countries: 18,562,994 in Egypt; 5,938,093 in Iraq before the U.S. attack; 18,319,328 in Iran; 35,770,928 in Pakistan; 18,882,272 in Turkey; and 64,046,149 in Indonesia. Thus, the combined number of military personnel from those armies is roughly 162 million, over three times that of the U.S., which has only 79 million (Wadjdi 2002). Considering this data, the fundamentalists compare the Muslim world to a giant sleeping tiger that is waiting for the right time to wake up. They are convinced that if the Muslim world unites, it will have the potential to create a new superpower, as a slogan on an *Al-Wa'ie* cover proclaims: "*Membangu Adidiaya Baru*" (Establishing the New Superpower!).

SYMBOLIC VIOLENCE

The idea of conflict resulting from the construction of the image of the Other as enemy does not necessarily imply physical violence. The fundamentalists' expression of this image is unique. For example, it is different from the racism in America at the turn of the nineteenth century, when white people could easily discriminate simply because of skin color. It is also different from that of the Dayaks in Sambas and Kalimantan during the conflict of 2000, where Maduranese could be killed because of their ethnicity.

It should be pointed out, however, that MMI and HTI do have an ideology similar to these two examples. Like the white people who saw black people as sub-human, or like the Dayaks who see Maduranese as colonialists taking what is rightfully theirs and who thereby feel justified in killing them, the fundamentalists see non-Muslims as uncivilized humans who are continually hostile to Islam. But the expression of this enmity takes a different form; while they might be harboring distrust and suspicion in their minds, their daily interactions with the Other are peaceful. Generally they are devoted Muslims, well known for being humble and polite, and for living a simple life. For example, if a Jew came to their office, they would not attack him/her, despite the hatred they might feel. They have moral injunctions regarding the use of violence. This paragraph from the Qur'an is enough to control them so that they do not attack the Other because of religious reasons.

> Allah forbids you not, with regard to those who fight you for [your] faith or drive you out of your homes, from dealing kindly and justly with them: for Allah loveth those who are just. Allah only forbids you, with regard to those who fight you for [your] faith, and drive you out of your homes, and support [Others] in driving you out, from turning to them [for friendship and protection]. It is such as turn to them [in these circumstances], that do wrong (Qur'an 60: 8–9).

Nevertheless, the categories of those who "fight you" and "drive you out of your homes," are flexible and open to interpretation. The commonly acknowledged feeling of being under siege and humiliated by the world's non-Muslim powers may lead some radical Muslim groups or individuals to categorize the current situation of Muslims in the world as "being fought" or "being driven out of their homes."

The continuous characterization of Islamic fundamentalism as violent, radical, and hard-line motivates leaders to emphasize their movement's nonviolence. This is reflected, for instance, in HTI's stated methods: namely, ideological (*fikriyah*), political (*siyasiyah*), and nonviolent (*la maadiyah*). Specifically, HTI spokesman Ismail Yusanto, referring to *dakwah* (the struggle to establish an Islamic state or apply Islamic law), states:

> Hizbut Tahrir is a *dakwah* movement that since its beginning has been committed to nonviolence (*la madiyah*), because Muhammad's *dakwah* to establish an Islamic state was without violence (Hizbut Tahrir 2003b).

In connection with this claim, HTI held a public seminar specifically aimed at countering the stigmatizing of fundamentalist Muslim groups, especially HTI, as prone to violence and terrorism. An HTI activist, Abu Haris Al-Amin, compared today's world with the time before the coming of Islam (*jahiliyah*). He argued that social transformation could not be accomplished by destroying non-Islamic (*kufr*) facilities, symbols, or places of sin. The reason is that non-Islamic social thought and ideology cannot be destroyed through physical power, but only by transforming people's feelings and thoughts into an Islamic way of life. Therefore, he repudiates violence in the struggle to establish an Islamic state.

He bases this argument on a *hadith* that says, ". . . the worst of your leaders are people whom you hate and who hate you. . . . We asked, oh Muhammad, should we raise our weapons if that happens? Muhammad answered, No, as long as they establish *sholat*." The term "establish *sholat*" is understood symbolically as establishment of the Islamic system. This *hadith*, then, is understood as permission to declare holy war (*jihad*) against a current secular government that does not establish the Islamic system. According to Al-Amin (Abu Haris), this argument is flawed because it ignores the fact (*tahqi al-manath*) that the *hadith* was addressed to a Muslim ruler within an Islamic state (*dar al-Islam*). This *hadith* should not be applied to a non-Islamic state (*dar al-kufr*). Thus, even when a government does not implement Islamic law or "establish *sholat*," Muslims are not allowed to declare *jihad* against it (Al-Amin 2003, 13–16).

Similarly, Irfan Awwas, head of MMI's executive board, emphasizes the nonviolent character of Islam:

> In its long history, Islam does not legalize and command doing violence to any people or on behalf of anything. Instead, it commands Muslims to do good deeds and justice to people, regardless of whether they are Muslims or non-Muslim. . . . The concepts of *amr ma'ruf* and *nahy mungkar* are not justification to do violence. They command Muslims to do good deeds to anyone and to struggle to stop any kind of evil deed (Awwas 2003).

Thus far there is no evidence that fundamentalists have destroyed discotheques or bars (*maksiat* or sinful places) as have FPI (Front Pembela Islam) and GPK (Gerakan Pemuda Ka'bah); these acts led to the characterization of fundamentalist Muslim groups as violent. HTI holds that *dakwah*, or the struggle to establish an Islamic state or apply Islamic law, must be done peacefully through what it calls ideological, political, and cultural means. In fact, HTI takes the method of Muhammad's *dakwah* in the Meccan period as a model. As the Islamic state had not yet been established in the Meccan period, Muhammad, according to HTI, never instigated physical confrontation with the *kafir* Quraish in Mecca. God's permission for *jihad* against non-Muslims was given only when Muhammad had attained political power in Medina.

Regarding MMI, its leaders do not deny the possibility of physical confrontation with people who impede their struggle to apply Islamic law, but they stipulate that it is necessary only when a physical attack has impeded their *dakwah*. The fight against obstacles to Islamic law, according to MMI, must be conducted uniformly. That is, they advocate fighting ideological attacks with ideological movements, political obstacles with political movements, and physical attacks with physical defense. It is for the purpose of that last obstacle, Irfan insisted, that MMI created Laskar Mujahidin (Mujahidin Troops), as well as for conducting *jihad* in battlefields like Ambon and Poso.

The obligation of *jihad*, according to MMI, only applies when Muslims are attacked, as in the cases of Ambon, Poso, Chechnya, Palestine, Iraq, Afghanistan, etc. The law of holy war itself, according to HTI, is limited to battlefields with the status of *fardlu 'ain* (individual obligation) for Muslims who live in conflict areas, and *fardlu kifayah* (group obligation) for all Muslims around the world. In addition, HTI holds that the law of holy war can be executed only by an Islamic state. Since there is no Islamic state yet, conduct of *jihad* individually or in a group is forbidden.

Do these claims provide enough proof that the fundamentalists are not violent? The answer to this question depends on the definition of violence. If violence is defined in its conventional meaning of acts that cause physical damage, such as homicide, ethnic cleansing, war crimes, destruction of physical facilities, or actions that cause psychological suffering such as expulsion, kidnapping, torture, and rape, then the fundamentalists do not engage in violence.[12]

On the other hand, examination of the fundamentalists' construction of the image of the enemy and their attitudes toward the Other calls to mind Pierre Bourdieu's theory of symbolic violence. Bourdieu, a French linguist, used this term to address the non-obvious violence resulting from the use of language by the dominant class in such way that this class unconsciously misconstrues domination as legitimate. Symbolic violence occurs when the dominated class accepts distorted symbols (concepts, ideas, precepts, beliefs, etc.), so that domination over them becomes permanent. The distorted symbols are developed through what Bourdieu calls monosignification or monosemy, so that the dominated class, without realizing it, accepts these distorted symbols as common sense.[13]

Bourdieu's explanation of symbolic violence refers to the connection between knowledge and power and a top-down relationship in which the dominant class is the actor of symbolic violence and the dominated class the victim. However, Bourdieu's ideas on monosignification or monosemy as the means of symbolic violence makes possible the extension of the meaning of symbolic violence. Symbolic violence does not refer solely to manipulation of language for the interests of power; it also refers to a mechanism for providing monolithic information or symbols for individual or group interest by discrediting the Other. The actor of symbolic violence creates distorted information, which is unconsciously accepted as legitimate. This actor can be anyone, not only someone from the ruling class, but also an ordinary person. A beggar, for example, can carry out symbolic violence by creating a false appearance so that the Other will feel guilty and thus give aid.

Referring to Bourdieu's theory of symbolic violence, the construction of the image of the enemy, especially in the four patterns developed by the fundamentalists, can also be recognized as a form of violence. Using Bourdieu's terminology, fundamentalists create monosignificant symbols by simultaneously emphasizing what they identify as non-Muslims' attacks on Islam throughout history and ignoring the cooperation and harmony between Muslims and non-Muslims. Like their counterpart, the u.s. government, which stigmatizes Islamic fundamentalism as evil, and like some orientalists who identify Islam as a war-like religion and Muslims as barbarous, the fundamentalists, in fact, have been doing the same thing. This unbalanced collection of information can accumulate in attitudes of confrontation, hatred, anger, suspicion, and resentment that will incite actual physical violence or what Erich Fromm has called "vengeful destructiveness."

Other examples of symbolic violence are the fundamentalists' depictions of the Other as constantly antagonistic and threatening toward Islam, as poor leaders or allies, and as continuously in conflict with Muslims. In this way the fundamentalists stigmatize the Other with these negative characteristics. They employ a rhetoric of violence in demonizing the Other through Islamophobic discourse, as already mentioned.

And, while the fundamentalists insist that they repudiate terrorism, their support for and idolization of those responsible for the October 12, 2002

Bali bombing could be understood as legitimizing terrorism. Many of Ba'asyir's students in Ngruki *pesantren*, MMI's base, grieved publicly over the corpse of Fathurahman Al-Ghozi, the suspected bomber of the U.S. embassy in the Philippines. Moreover, even though MMI points to Qur'anic restrictions of *jihad*, the MMI website published a *fatwa* (juristic opinion) of Dr. Abdullah Azzam that inflames the spirit of holy war in Muslim fundamentalists worldwide. Quoting two provocative verses of the Qur'an (9:36, 5) that command Muslims to battle *kafir*, Azzam emphasizes the obligation of all Muslims around the world to take part in holy war:

Oh preacher . . . there is no value for you to be outside in the heat of the sun, except if you raise your weapons and attack the *thaghut* and *kafir*.

Look for death, you will get life. Make your houses lions' cages, don't make your houses into places to raise sheep that will be slaughtered by *thaghut*.[14]

Furthermore, MMI often publishes inflammatory speeches of Osama bin Laden urging Muslims to fight non-Islamic powers, especially the United States. In his court defense, Ba'asyir refused to be linked with Osama, but claimed he had a faith network with him through the universal brotherhood of Islam. He quoted Osama's letter encouraging Muslims to *jihad* and to fight America.

This examination of the way in which fundamentalists construct the image of the enemy and its relation to symbolic violence make it difficult to believe their claims of being nonviolent. Violence can be found not only in actions, but also in words and discourse.[15]

FLAWS IN THE FUNDAMENTALIST ARGUMENTS

Critiquing the Four-Fold Discourse

The fundamentalists' verbal and visual constructions of the image of the enemy are problematical not only because of their implicit violence, but also because their discourse patterns are fraught with inherent weaknesses.

Ideologization, as we have seen, focuses not only on cases of Muslim versus non-Muslim nuanced conflict, such as that between Israel and Palestine and the Muslim-Christian conflict in Ambon, but also on conflicts completely without religious nuances, such as those in Aceh and Sambas (Kalimantan), and even loans from international monetary institutions. The fundamentalists' analyses of these cases are based on totally irrelevant arguments. For example, they cite the presence of Muslim victims in Aceh as evidence of an anti-Islamic conspiracy behind the conflict. This argument is irrelevant because most Acehnese happen to be Muslim, as are most other Indonesians. Another example is Irfan S. Awwas's accusation of Hasan Tiro, the leader of GAM who moved to Sweden, of being a convert to Judaism; the conflict began long before he moved to Sweden. Moreover, there is no evidence to support fundamentalists' claims that the involvement of foreign institutions, principally the Henry Dunant Center (HDC), is a non-Muslim attempt to weaken Muslim countries. Today such foreign involvement is normal in conflict areas, not only in Muslim countries but also in non-Muslim countries, like Yugoslavia and Rwanda.

Another flawed argument is the claim that the clash between the Maduranese and the Dayaks in Sambas, Kalimantan in 2000 was a religious conflict. Fundamentalists base their argument on the fact that the Madurese victims were Muslims. The victims' religion is inconsequential because this conflict had nothing to do with Islam versus non-Islam; rather it was an *ethnic* conflict between Madurese and Dayaks that was complicated by economic rivalry.

Still another invalid argument is the fundamentalists' identification of foreign loans from international monetary institutions such as the IMF,

World Bank, and CGI to Indonesia as part of a non-Muslim scheme to control Muslim countries. In fact, loans like these were given not only to Muslim countries, but also to other developing countries including Argentina, Brazil, and Thailand. The truth is that foreign loans control underdeveloped and developing countries in general, not Muslim countries specifically.

Finally, fundamentalists argue that Pancasila is part of Zionist infiltration into a Muslim country. Such an accusation is painful for most Indonesians who are proud of Pancasila as the result of their founding fathers' effort to unite Indonesia's diverse population.

Demonization, the second pattern used by the fundamentalists in creating the image of the enemy, is also open to criticism. A simplistic example is Abu Bakar Ba'asyir's characterization of non-Muslims (*kafir*) as visible Satans, likening them to the devil, the unseen Satan. No less naive is the fundamentalists' sweeping analysis of the secular system's failure. As proof, they cite not only the permissiveness, crime, divorce, abortion, and HIV/AIDS in Western countries; they also include the deep-rooted corruption, collusion, nepotism, regional autonomy policy, and natural disasters like floods and drought in Indonesia. In so doing they ignore the progress of Western countries and the welfare benefits in other countries like Japan, China, South Korea, Cuba, and Malaysia that use a secular system. Equally flawed is their simplistic argument that implementation of Islamic law will solve every problem, as points of Islamic law are debatable and subject to interpretation. The only time in history that Islamic law was implemented was the time of the Islamic empire, and this law was subject to change depending on the caliph in power. Most Islamic governments, like Saudi Arabia, Afghanistan (before the U.S. attack), and Pakistan (before 1998), are authoritarian and have a low index of health, income, education, life expectancy, and gender equality.

In the third discourse pattern of sweeping emphasis on the so-called inevitable clash between Islam and other civilizations, fundamentalists cite U.S. foreign policies that oppress Muslim countries as evidence of this clash. In fact, U.S. foreign policies oppress not only Muslim but also non-Muslim countries, such as North Korea and Cuba. And what Bush called the "axis of evil" included not only the Muslim countries of Iran and Iraq, but also North Korea.

Current global politics also call into question the supposed polarization of Muslims with the rest of the world. The demonstrations against global capitalism and resistance to the developed countries of the European Union at the 2003 WTO meeting in Cancun, Mexico, for example, were much more broadly based. Moreover, even among developed countries there have been periodic, heated disputes, as evidenced by the refusal of France, Germany, and Russia to participate in the U.S. attack on Iraq. The idea that non-Muslims are a single community is absurd because ideology is not the only consideration in a state's foreign policy. China, a communist state, cooperates with the U.S. for economic interests. In the past these two countries were allied in the Iran-Iraq war. Obviously, when need arises, Muslim and non-Muslim countries will work together just as any other sovereign states do.

As for the fourth discourse pattern of imagining Islam's victory through the revival of the Islamic caliphate, if the fundamentalists' prediction of the downfall of global capitalism's hegemony is not an illusion, this is good news for the people in the world who fight for a more balanced global order. However, the fundamentalists' imagining of Islam as a new superpower is frightening for both non-Muslims and liberal Muslims. Many people hope for the establishment of a more balanced global order rather than the emergence of Islam as a new superpower, fearing that the latter would create new forms of injustice. They are particularly concerned that Islamic concepts of leadership and apostasy would create discrimination against non-Muslims. In addition, the fundamentalists' calculation of the Muslim world's military potential creates fear of the possibility of war and violence in the struggle to establish their goal.

Another Flawed Argument: Perpetual Conflict

Apart from using the four discourse patterns discussed above in developing the image of the enemy, fundamentalists also make exaggerated and oversimplified arguments concerning perpetual conflict. For some people, the contemporary issue of terrorism, which has had a wide impact on the Muslim world, is compatible with this notion. Many scholars argue that events of the twenty-first century, especially since the 9/11 tragedy, demonstrate an ongoing collision between Islam and the rest of the world, especially the West. Samuel Huntington has argued that the events of September 11 represent an episode in the long and protracted struggle between two very different civilizations—the West and Islam (El Fadl 2002, 3). Richard Falk, a Princeton University scholar, has argued that in the age of globalization there is a deliberate attempt to "exclude" Muslims from the community of world civilizations—to make them pariahs, non-persons (as quoted by Ahmed 2003, 20). Historical evidence shows that Islam has had confrontations with all other major world religions: Judaism in the Middle East; Christianity in the Balkans, Nigeria, Sudan, the Philippines, and Indonesia; Hinduism in South Asia; Buddhism in China; and even communism. The current conflicts in Chechnya and China can be seen as further evidence.

However, there are also numerous situations around the world that belie the fundamentalists' notion of perpetual conflict between Islam and non-Islam. Their argument that Muslims throughout the world are humiliated and oppressed is contradicted in light of Ahmed's calculations that one-third of the world's 1.3 billion Muslims live in non-Muslim countries; about 25 million, who live in 55 countries, coexist with non-Muslims in the West, including seven million in the United States and two million in the United Kingdom, countries that fundamentalists consider to be the heartland of infidels (house of war) or *dar al-harb* (Ahmed 2003, 7). While Muslims were being persecuted in Iraq and elsewhere, they could practice their faith freely and flourish in the United States, the United Kingdom, and other non-Muslim countries (Ahmed 2003, 17).

The above facts also counter fundamentalists' boasts about the greatness of the Islamic state when they argue that non-Muslims were able to live peacefully under Muslim rule in medieval Spain, as opposed to the oppression that Muslims have endured under non-Muslim rulers. Even though there have been sporadic instances of discrimination against Muslims in the West, these are likely to have been caused by a misunderstanding of Islam, long associated with violence, and to have been committed by individuals rather than by explicit governmental policy. The fundamentalists' belief in the nature of non-Muslims as being totally antagonistic toward Islam can never be proven satisfactorily.

In addition, the fundamentalists' contention regarding the humiliation endured by Muslims around the world contradicts the fact that several Muslim countries including Qatar, the United Arab Emirates, Kuwait, and Saudi Arabia have some of the highest per capita incomes in the world (*Pocket World in Figures*, 26).

The disasters that befell Muslims in Palestine, Bosnia, Kosovo, Chechnya, Ambon, Poso, Afghanistan, Iraq, and so forth are saddening, not only for Muslims but also for humanity in a way that goes beyond religion. To see these tragedies as examples of the anti-Islamic nature of non-Muslims, however, is naive and exaggerated. In fact, ideological factors, local politics, and social and economic situations are the complicating issues of these conflicts. The problem of nationality, for instance, is a determinant in the Israeli-Palestinian conflict; social and economic clashes incited the Christian-Muslim conflict in the Moluccas; separatism is the main factor of the Russia-Chechnya conflict, and so on. Moreover, there are abundant examples of Muslims and non-Muslims coexisting within conflict areas.

The fundamentalists' strong suspicions and distrust of the Other are hard to accept. In a recorded preaching, Abu Bakr Ba'asyir expressed distrust of non-Muslims cooperating with Muslims because, for him, the *kafir* character is essentially hostile toward Islam. Thus, he feels, Muslims should rule non-Muslims in order to control this hostility. Yet there are many examples of non-Muslims helping and cooperating to ensure Muslims' rights: the u.s. military rescued Bosnian Muslims from

Serbian ethnic cleansing, in India a vast number of Muslims coexist with Hindus despite the conflict in Kashmir, and in the Moluccas Muslims and non-Muslims worked together to create peace through the Malino Agreement. Despite the intense conflict between Palestine and Israel, there are also many stories about Jews defending the Palestinians and about cooperation between Jews and Muslims to resolve this conflict. There were, for example, Jews who protested Ariel Sharon's anti-Palestine policies, Israeli air force personnel who refused to bomb civilian houses, and Israeli and Palestinian non-governmental organizations that met in Amman to discuss Israeli-Palestinian conflict resolution (*Tempo* 2003b and 2003a). Recently the world also witnessed constructive cooperation between Muslims and non-Muslims in defending the Muslim world, as shown by the cooperation between Muslim and leftist groups in England demonstrating against the war in Iraq. (*The Economist* 2003, 55). Many countries in the West, a bloc that fundamentalists identify as the heart of the anti-Islam conspiracy, were the first to help Iranian earthquake victims in December 2003.

The fundamentalists' simplistic division is also shown to be invalid when looking at the internal conflicts based on ethnicity within Muslim societies. Examples include strife between the Northern Alliance and the Taliban in Afghanistan, Kurds in Iraq versus Turkey, Saddam Hussein versus Kurds in Iraq before the u.s. attack, traditional Muslims versus Jema'ah Ahmadiyah in some places in Indonesia, and the repression of Anwar Ibrahim by Mahathir Muhammad in Malaysia, to mention a few. Thus, the fundamentalists' argument, when closely analyzed, does not hold water.

Neither is the feeling valid of being under siege by a united non-Muslim global conspiracy. After September 11, 2001, not only fundamentalist Muslims, but *all* Muslims have felt under siege by Bush's war on terrorism. The sense of being under siege, to a certain extent, is understandable because of the frequent persecution of Muslims throughout history. But to see Islam as the only society under siege is not acceptable because many people in the third world, including those in non-Muslim countries in Latin America and Africa, also feel under siege by globalization and Westernization. Indeed very few of the nations that have the highest foreign debt and that are the largest recipients of aid are Muslim countries—Indonesia, Pakistan, Syria, Lebanon, Iran, and Egypt, and Turkey; the rest are non-Muslim countries (*Pocket World in Figures*, 38–40). Thus, Ahmed was right when he said that violence is routine and it can happen to anyone regardless of their religion (Ahmed 2003, 17).

Misleading Selections from Religious Texts

As in a war or other conflict situation, perceptions of the opposing party are usually based on oversimplified and non-objective arguments and stories. Even when stories and arguments are true, they are spiced with provocative and non-compromising language aimed at developing the image of the Other as enemy. This image can become even more powerful when negative aspects of the Other are emphasized and positive aspects are ignored. The continuous internalization of this image of the enemy can instill anger, hatred, resentment, suspicion, distrust, and hostility.

In this way the fundamentalists' image of the enemy is based on misleading interpretations of Qur'anic verses and *hadiths* by using the fourfold discourse pattern of enmity discussed earlier. They have selected more than fifty texts from the Qur'an and *hadiths* that convey confrontational ideas of the Other. The bulk of these are listed below.

1. Perpetual conflict between Islam and non-Islam (Qur'an 7: 16-17; 4: 76; 4: 101)
2. The nature of non-Muslims' mortal enmity toward Islam (Qur'an 3: 118; 2: 120, 217; 5: 82)
3. The Jews' hatred of Islam (Qur'an 3: 118)
4. Non-Muslims' conspiracy against Islam (Qur'an 8: 15, 30 86)
5. *Kafirs'* wicked intentions toward Islam (Qur'an 2: 102, 109; 8: 30; 8: 36; 5: 110; 6: 7, 10, 13, 27, 76; 34: 43; 46: 7; 61: 8; a *hadith* that describes

Muslims as food that is torn apart by hungry wolves as a metaphor for enemy nations surrounding Islam

6. Collaboration among non-Muslims against Islam (Qur'an 8: 73)
7. The superiority of Islam over all other religions (Qur'an 3: 19, 85)
8. Prohibition against taking non-Muslims as leaders, allies, or protectors (Qur'an 3: 28; 4: 144, 159; 5: 51; 60: 1)
9. The command to have a firm attitude toward non-Muslims and to fight those who battle Islam or refuse to submit to a Muslim ruler (Qur'an 2: 190, 191, 193; 4: 75; 8: 60; 9: 29, 73, 123; 48: 29)
   The victory of Islam over all other religions (Qur'an 10: 103; 24: 55; *hadith* on the spread of Islam throughout the world)

This selection of verses is misleading because when they are understood literally and regarded as the Qur'an's final position towards the Other, they contradict the general Qur'anic discourse of the Other. Examination of this general discourse suggests that the Qur'an teaches respect for and acceptance of the Other. Although in many places the Qur'an criticizes non-Muslims, as in the verses referred to by the fundamentalists, this does not signify total rejection and confrontation. The following verses demonstrate how the Qur'an repeatedly admits, accepts, and respects diversity, stating that diversity is God's will.

> We have revealed to you the book with the truth, verifying that which is before it of the book and a guardian over it. So judge between them by what Allah has revealed and follow not their desires, [turning away] from the truth that has come unto you. For every one of you we have appointed a divine law and traced a way out. And if Allah had pleased, He would have made you a single *ummah*, but that he try you in what he gave you. So vie with one another in virtuous deeds. To Allah you will all return, so He will inform you of what wherein you differed (Qur'an 5: 48).

Similarly the Qur'an says:

If God had so wanted, He could have made them a single people. But He admits whom He wills to His grace and, for the wrongdoers there will be no protector nor helper (Qur'an 42: 8).

To every community, We appointed acts of devotion, which they observe, so let them not dispute with you in the matter, and call to your Lord. Surely you are on a right guidance (Qur'an 22; 67).

The Qur'an not only accepts diversity, but it also justifies the possibility of other religions as valid ways to salvation, as stated in the following two, rather similar, verses.

Those who believe in God [in the Qur'an] and those who follow the Jewish [scripture], and the Christians and Sabians, any who believe in God and the last day, and work shall have their reward with their Lord: on them shall be no fear, nor shall they grieve (Qur'an 2: 62).

Those who believe [in the Qur'an], those who follow the Jewish [scripture], and the Sabians and the Christians and whoever believes in God and the last day and works righteously; on them shall be no fear, nor shall they grieve (Qur'an 5: 72).

The Qur'anic criticisms of some non-Muslims for their negative attitudes toward Muslims (see, for example, Qur'an 2: 120, 217; 3: 118; 62: 6) do not apply to non-Muslims in general. For instance, while the Qur'an warns Muhammad of the enmity of the Jews and the polytheists, it also reminds him about the kindness of the Christians:

The strongest among men in enmity to the believers wilt thou find the Jews and Pagans; and nearest among them in love to the believers wilt thou find those who say, "We are Christians," because amongst these are men devoted to learning and men who have renounced the world, and they are not arrogant (Qur'an 5: 82).

In other places, the Qur'an rejects the generalization that all others are hostile to Muslims. It explicitly recognizes the kindness and righteousness of the Other, both socially and spiritually:

> Not all of them are alike; among them is a group who stands for the right and keeps nights reciting the words of Allah and prostrate themselves in adoration before Him. They have faith in Allah and in the last day; they enjoin what is good and forbid what is wrong, and vie one with another in good deeds. And those are among the righteous (Qur'an 4: 113).

> And whatever good they do, they will not be denied it. And Allah knows those who keep their duty (Qur'an 93: 112–4).

The discerning nature of Qur'anic attitudes toward the Other is also reflected in discourses on the Other that are always followed by qualifying phrases, such as "from among them" (Q. 3: 75), "many among them" (Q. 2: 109, 5: 66, 22: 17, 57: 26), "most of them" (Q. 2: 105, 7: 102, 10: 36), "some of them" (Q. 2: 145), and "a group among them" (Q. 3: 78).

Other Qur'anic verses that convey criticism (not confrontation) of the Other should be read within the overall historical context of the particular revelation. Ignorance of the socio-historical context of the particular text, according to Farid Esack, a liberal South African Muslim scholar, will support generalized denunciation and rejection of the Other and confusion between passages expressing confrontation and respectful recognition. According to Esack's hermeneutics, the Qur'anic attitude toward the Other is varied because of the variety of people Muhammad encountered and their responses to Qur'anic messages.

> The Qur'anic position toward the other unfolded gradually in terms of their varied responses to the message of Islam and to the prophetic presence. Any view to the contrary would invariably lead to the conclusion that Qur'an presents a confused and contradictory view of the other. The idea of the gradual and contextual development of the Qur'anic position towards the

other has significant implications. One cannot speak of a final Qur'anic position towards the other, secondly, it is wrong to apply texts of opprobrium in a universal manner to all whom one chooses to define as "people of the book," "disbelievers," etc. and in a historical fashion (Esack 1997, 148–49).

Esack examined various aspects of Qur'anic discourse on the Other and suggests an understanding of the Qur'anic attitude towards the other based on the socio-historical context. First, the Qur'an rarely uses the nouns *kafiru/kuffar*, which in English are equivalent to "non-Muslim" or "disbeliever." Instead, it employs descriptive phrases such as *alladhina amanu* (literally meaning "those who are convinced") and *'alladhina kafaru* (literally meaning "those who deny/reject/are ungrateful"). These descriptive phrases, according to Esack, "express specific nuances in the text that indicate a particular level of faith conviction or denial or rejection or ingratitude." In addition, some of these terms are used interchangeably, e.g. *muslimun* and *mu'minun* or "people of the book" and "Christians" or "Jews."

Second, aside from terms of opprobrium such as *kafir*, *munafiq*, and *mushrik*, other terms are rarely used in a negative or positive manner without qualification. In addition, the terms *kufr* and *shirk* are also used by the Qur'an to describe reprehensible acts committed by some of those within the Muslim or believing community (Qur'an 39: 7.) Third, the terms of opprobrium are not always addressed to historical, religious, or social groupings, but are also addressed to individuals, including the self-righteous and hypocrites. In the same way the term *muslim*, in its various forms, is invoked to refer to both individuals and to the characteristic of submission as found in individuals, groups, or even inanimate objects (Esack 1999, 70).

Therefore, the generalization of non-Muslims as characteristically antagonistic toward Muslims is not only absurd; it is also an abuse of the Qur'an. Being non-Muslim is not evil and does not presuppose hatred and enmity, as the fundamentalists claim. Belief and behavior, according to Esack, "are not genetic elements such as the colour of one's eyes in supposedly homogeneous and unchanging communities." Qur'anic condemnation and criticism of the Other, Esack maintains, is not based simply on being non-Muslim (in terms of embracing institutionalized Islam), but rather on the Qur'anic vision of the struggle to establish an order based on divine unity (*tawhid*), justice, and *islam* (submission to God). The confrontational Qur'anic discourses on the Other are much more directed toward fighting religious claims that justify "exploitative practices of tribal chauvinism" (Esack 1999, 72).

FUNDAMENTALISM AS A RESISTANCE MOVEMENT

There is still another significant facet of fundamentalism that needs to be emphasized. Although most Muslims are aware that the fundamentalists' discourse on conflict and violence is incompatible with efforts to create peaceful coexistence in a pluralistic society, many admire Islamic fundamentalism as a resistance movement against global capitalism. In her book, *World on Fire: How Exporting Free Market Democracy Breeds Ethnic Hatred and Global Instability*, Amy Chua describes Islamic fundamentalism as a movement of hatred against a "market dominant minority." Regardless of its violent and deluded character, Islamic fundamentalism, according to Chua, offers an alternative to the humiliation caused by global capitalism. Fundamentalism, in her view, creates global instability and provides "a scapegoat, a mission, an identity, and chance for the powerless to regain power" (Chua 2003, 158).

Similarly, Eko Prasetyo views Islamic fundamentalism, or what he calls "the defenders of God," as an exotic social movement that offers certainty for an alienated society and hope for the hopeless and despondent. Fundamentalism functions to assuage nostalgia for the idea of a heaven that has been lost, and that will return only in a situation where many people feel alienated by modernity's materialism and individualism. In a setting where the downtrodden are depressed by the high rate of unemployment, the rise of corruption, and by a legal system that cannot address people's demands for justice, the idea of implementing Islamic law is an attractive alternative. Islamic fundamentalism provides a new imagination that is necessary to fight against other fundamentalisms, most notably "market fundamentalism." (Prasetyo 2002, 56). It is in this context of struggle that the fundamentalists' image of the enemy can be understood and respected. According to James Aho, this is needed in a conflict situation that provides the spirit and orientation to fight. Even in a situation when the enemy is absent, the invention of an enemy is necessary (Aho 1994, 23).

The attractiveness of the fundamentalists' claims is evident in the healthy sales of their publications; they appear to offer an alternative ideology that finds its own market in Indonesia. Most of the books published by Wihdah Press have been sold out and reprinted several times. Likewise, *Al-Islam* bulletins, which are distributed to mosques every Friday, are always in high demand.

Although the fundamentalists have been characterized as exclusive and violent, their activities seem to be enthusiastically welcomed. Most HTI public programs I observed were attended by crowds of over five hundred. But this fact by itself does not necessarily mean that these groups have strong support; people bought their publications and attended their programs for various reasons, including curiosity. Many people were curious about the fundamentalist movement when it became popular because of the globalization of the terrorism issue. However, the success of the publishing program at least demonstrates that fundamentalists have their own market and resonance. Just as John L. Esposito pointed out that the wide distribution of Samuel Huntington's books demonstrated the "market for clash"; similarly, the fundamentalists also have found a market for their ideology of conflict (Esposito 2002, 126).

The fundamentalists' attraction, apart from offering an alternative to a dying society unable to rid itself of powerlessness and humiliation, also derives from HTI's ability to create a humble, altruistic, simple, and intellectual image of itself. These qualities can draw sympathy from people who are tired of the elite's arrogance and corruption and the politicians' hedonistic and wealthy lifestyles.

MMI's style, by contrast, is brash and angry. While there is no evidence that MMI members have committed acts of violence, their manner can arouse suspicion of violence, especially because of the involvement of some Al-Mukmin *pesantren* alumni as MMI's base and the home of some terrorists. MMI regularly holds academic seminars and dialogues regarding the legacy of the application of Islamic law in Indonesia, but its members tend to do so using the rhetoric of violence. Laskar Mujahidin's militaristic appearance strengthens this suspicion.

Even though the terrorism issue tends to associate the fundamentalists with violence, at the same time it increases their popularity. Because the issue was propagated by America under Bush, whose arrogance evokes hatred from many parts of the world, the fundamentalists are seen as heroes and symbols of resistance against global hegemony.

Voices empathetic to the fundamentalists confirm the thesis that injustice, when combined with extremist ideology, can breed fundamentalism and radicalism. Most MMI and HTI followers are not poor; in fact they are middle-class, urban, and educated. It is true that poverty breeds fundamentalism, but not in the simple meaning of lack of food and other basic needs. The fundamentalists are the middle class that feels impoverished and disempowered by the unbalanced global order driven by neo-liberalism and Pax Americana. Thus, despite the confrontational attitudes and violent characteristics exhibited by the fundamentalists, they have also presented themselves as an attractive alternative, an ideology of protest.

But this alone may not be enough to ensure future growth for MMI and HTI, as there are numerous obstacles generated by their own ways of operating. Their oversimplified arguments, for example, in the end are likely to be counterproductive because those who have access to more balanced information would find their logic difficult to accept. Another obstacle to growth comes from the fundamentalists' totalitarian ideology. The strict and non-compromising character of their struggle to implement Islamic law is not likely to be accepted in Indonesian culture, which is different from Arabic culture. Unlike Arabia, as the center of the Islamic caliphate's past glory, Indonesian society does not have an image of the past glory of Islam. What it has, instead, is the memory of the past glory of an ethnic-Islamic kingdom with pluralistic and accommodative characteristics. Pancasila, the state ideology, appears to be more accepted as the ideology of multi-ethnic and multi-religious Indonesia. Pancasila is an invention of a form of Islam native to Indonesia and is accepted by most Indonesian Muslims.

While the majority of Indonesian Muslims identify themselves as Islamic, this feeling of identity does not reduce their sense of nationalism, and the two coexist. The history of political Islam in Indonesia also proves the nationalistic character of most Indonesian Muslims. The Islamic political parties in Indonesia have never gotten more than 37.5 percent of the vote. This figure includes PKB (Nation Awakening Party) and PAN (National Mandate Party), which are reluctant to be identified as Islamic parties (Effendi 2003, 214).

The fundamentalists cite the experience of several regions in Indonesia, such as Aceh and several districts in West Java, as proof of Muslims' nostalgia for Islamic law. However, the truth is that these attempts at implementing Islamic law have failed even with the political support of the regional governments. The few bills that do implement certain aspects of Islamic law are superficial regulations, such as putting Islamic names on the roads and implementing a curfew. Meanwhile, in broader aspects, secular criminal law is still used.

With a strict and non-compromising ideology, especially the idea of excluding non-Muslims as leaders and allies, the fundamentalists, in fact, limit the opportunity to develop a stronger resistance movement against global capitalism and Pax Americana. While the fundamentalists take global capitalism as the enemy, the anti-globalist movement is actually supported primarily by non-Muslim groups and individuals, not only in poor and developing countries, but also in Europe and North America. In fact, defense of and support for Muslims' rights have often come from non-Muslim peace activists. Two years ago an English journalist died in the hospital because of Israeli army gunshot wounds suffered from his willingness to be a living barrier for Palestinian children. This is an example for the fundamentalists to consider. Being non-Muslim does not equate with being evil.

The dilemma of adopting either compromising or ideal strategies seems to have caused an unresolved internal difference among the fundamentalists. This dilemma rests on the strategy of either participating in the secular system or separating from it in the attempt to implement Islamic law. The debate on this issue has been unresolved for a long time even within MMI, which officially participates in the secular system. Many MMI activists were opposed to having their officials send a draft of an

Indonesian constitution and criminal code based on Islamic law to the Indonesian government and parliament.

This dilemma is also reflected in HTI's advocacy of implementing Islamic law, rather than an Islamic caliphate, as it formerly advocated. Many HTI and MMI activists admit that this issue has been a serious problem in the struggle to establish an Islamic system in Indonesia. In a conversation in the Wihdah Press office, an MMI activist expressed regret that the difficulty in uniting Muslims' visions is a serious obstacle to establishing Islamic law in Indonesia. This internal difference could also impede the fundamentalists' further growth.

History has shown that efforts to establish an Islamic state or Islamic law have always had to face the power and nationalistic sentiment of Indonesia, which is multi-ethnic and multi-religious. Indeed, compromise and collaboration are traditional Indonesian characteristics. In order for the fundamentalists to expand their base, they will need to compromise and to re-conceptualize their mission and strategy. Without such revision, they take the risk of being sidelined, as has happened in the past.

SUMMARY AND CONCLUSIONS

Examination of the two fundamentalist Muslim groups in Yogyakarta, Majelis Mujahidin Indonesia (MMI) and Hizbut Tahrir Indonesia (HTI), primarily through their publications and leaders' speeches, shows that they have been systematically constructing the image of the Other (that is, the non-Muslim world) as enemy. This process is obvious from their identification of and attitudes toward the Other, which include hatred, suspicion, anger, and resentment.

The fundamentalists are consumed by a totalitarian view of the Islamic system's superiority—an idea that divides the world simplistically into two opposing halves, Islamic and non-Islamic. This mindset consists of three elements: 1) an emphasis on confrontational passages of the Qur'an and *hadiths* that describe the endless animosity of non-Muslims toward Islam, 2) a feeling of being under attack coupled with distrust of *kafir* in friendships or alliances, and 3) attention to the perpetual conflict between Muslims and non-Muslims and insistence that it can cease only by non-Muslim submission to a Muslim ruler or Islamic law under the status of *dhimmi*.

Fundamentalists fortify this theologically based consciousness with references to historical events, identified as non-Muslim attacks on Islam, both physically and ideologically. Physical attacks refer to conflicts between Muslims and non-Muslims both in the past and currently. Ideological attacks, or what fundamentalists call the battle of ideas (*ghazw al-fikr/al siro' al-fikr*), refer to the imposition of modern ideologies, such as nationalism, orientalism, Christianization, capitalism, and secularism.

The fundamentalists use four discourse patterns that contribute greatly to the development of enmity in a way that could incite antagonistic attitudes toward the Other. In R. C. Mitchell's theory of conflict, this kind of discourse functions to group people into binary instinct categories of "us" and "them," thereby creating a "positive own-party image," and downgrading the Other.

The first discourse pattern, ideologization, includes emphasizing the anti-Islamic aspects of conflict and social analysis, stressing the failure of secular systems compared to the possible and hoped-for successes of the Islamic system, and creating anti-Islamic symbolic words and pictures. The second discourse pattern, demonization, is manifested in images depicting the Other as threatening, cruel, barbarous, and uncivilized. The third pattern, insistence on the so-called inevitable clash between Islam and non-Islam, is based on fundamentalists' belief in the superiority of Islamic rule and its complete contradiction of any other system. It leads to a refusal to share, compromise, or dialogue with other systems for governing the world. The fourth pattern, imagining the coming victory of Islam, foresees capitalism's imminent collapse and the rise of Islam as the world's superpower.

Although the fundamentalists develop an image of the Other as enemy, it does not necessarily cause problems or confrontations in their daily relationships with the Other. Neither do they engage in violence in physical terms. The fundamentalists insist that their movements are academic and nonviolent, and their actions seem to be consistent with their claims. Thus, the conflict resulting from the image of the enemy they construct is much more discursive than actual. Their production of the image of the Other as enemy, however, contributes to what Pierre Bourdieu called "symbolic violence" or what De Lauretis described as "rhetoric violence." This type of violence consists of a monolithic and non-objective discourse, creating a generalizing stigmatization of the Other, and making provocative statements against the other, all of which ultimately can lead to the potential for conflict and physical violence.

The fundamentalists' construction of the image of the enemy can best be understood in the context of conflict, wherein the image of the enemy is created to instill a fighting spirit and to foster the belief that one's own group is superior. In this context, the image of the enemy is based on oversimplified and irrelevant stories and arguments. Examination of Qur'anic general discourses shows that it not only accepts and respects the Other, but also justifies the Other. The contemporary life of Muslims and the state of world politics also prove the naiveté of the stories and arguments that the fundamentalists use to support the fourfold pattern.

Many Muslims are sympathetic to the fundamentalists as a way of resisting the hegemony of global capitalism but they do not support their agendas. While the groups have their own market, there are serious obstacles to their further growth. One is the irrelevant and oversimplified nature of their arguments, which are counterproductive because Indonesian society is religiously and ethnically plural. Another obstacle stems from their non-compromising paradigm regarding enforcing Islamic law or establishing an Islamic caliphate. The third obstacle comes from internal conflicts and differences among the fundamentalists, especially between the idealists and the pragmatists.

In conclusion, while this research on the construction of the image of the Other as enemy by fundamentalists has necessarily led to a negative impression of the proponents, it does not ignore the possibility that their critique can be helpful, or that the worldview demonstrated in their writings and activities can be valuable. Further research on MMI and HTI and on Islamic fundamentalism in general should be encouraged. Such research would examine not only fundamentalist perceptions of and attitudes toward the Other, but also the causes of these perceptions, particularly the international politics and economics that contribute to the radicalizing of society.

NOTES

1 For an analysis of the post-New Order resurgence of Islamic fundamentalism, see Zada 2002.

2 Responsibility Report of *Ahl al-Hal wal 'Ahd, Majelis Mujahidin Indonesia.*

3 See *Menganal Majelis Mujahidin: Untuk Penegakkan Syari'at Islam* (The Council of Mujahidin for Islamic Law Enforcement). n.d.

4 Kartosuwiryo was captured and executed by the army in 1962.

5 See MMI, *Usulan Amandemen UUD '45* and *Usulan Undang-Undang Hukum Pidana Republik Indonesia Disesuaikan dengan Syari'at Islam.* However, although this strategy is currently being undertaken, it is still debated among members of MMI. Some participants of the second Mujahidin congress in September, 2003 in Solo questioned why the officials of MMI sent the proposed draft of amendments to UUD '45 and the proposed criminal laws based on Islamic laws to the MPR, DPR, and the president, which are elements of the *kufr* system.

6 *Takbir* is proclaimed during political meetings and demostrations as a political exclamation or sloganeering in reference to Islam as a political ideology. The leader of the crowd shouts, *"Takbir!"* meaning "Declare greatness!" and the crowd responds with *"Allah Akbar!"* "God is greatest!"

7 To emphasize the anti-Islam aspect of this conflict, they refer to two *hadiths* when Muhammad warned Muslims about a battle that Muslims will fight in spreading Islam in the land of the Hindus. These *hadiths* state:

> Rasulullah saw promises that we will conquer the Hind land. If we find that Hind land, I will sacrifice my life and wealth. And if I am killed, I will be member of Syuhada'. (If I am not killed) I will [come] back, I am Abu Hurairah, the liberator (Nasai).

> There are two groups of my people whom Allah protected from the fire of Hell, (namely) a group that will conquer the Hind and a group that will be together with Jesus, the son of Mary" (Nasai). See Hizabut Tahrir 2001g and 2002d.

8 Hizbut Tahrir 2001f. MMI, through Wihdah Press, published several books about conflict in Ambon, including three books of Rustam Kasto: *Kospirasi Politik RMS dan Kristen Menghancurkan Ummat Islam di Maluku dan Ambon, Suara Maluku Membantah Rustam Kastor Menjawab*, and *Badai Pembalasan Laskar Mujahidin Ambon dan Maluku.*

9 For resources on these non-physical attacks, see Hizbut Tahrir 1996, 1999c, 2000c, 2001a, and 2001h; Iskandar 2001a; Zallum 2001; Sajid 2001b; Sajidah and Khatimah 2001; Thahan 2001; Nuaim Hidayat 2002; Al-Jawi 2003, 36.

10 The term "*Salib-Davidian*" (adjectival form of the cross and Star of David) is taken from a headline of *Sabili*. Similar terms, like "Zionis" and "Salibis" are frequently used in the fundamentalists' publications.

11 Huntington identified Confucianism and Islam as threats to Western civilization as he stated, "the most prominent form of this cooperation is the Confucian-Islamic connection that has emerged to challenge Western interests, values and power." See Huntington 1993, 22–49.

12 Jamil Salmi (2003) identifies it as direct violence compared to other kinds, such as violence by omission, mediated violence, repressive violence, and alienative violence.

13 For this kind of adaptation of Bourdieu's theory of symbolic violence, see Yasraf Amir Piliang, "Bahasa, Politik, dan Nasionalisme (1)," http://www.pikiran-rakyat. com.cetak/0902/05/khazanah/, and Imanol Galfarsoro, "Symbolic Violence and Linguistic Habitus in Pierre Bourdieu: An Instance of the 'Language is Power' View Revisited," http://www.ibslgu.ac.uk/forum/bourdieuBOURDIEU/.

14 Wasiat Asy-Syahid, Dr. Abdullah Azzam, http://www.majelis.mujahidin.or.id.

15 Al-Anshari 2002, 118–120. MMI also translated and published a book that contains a forward by Osama bin Laden, originally published by the Institute for Islamic Study and Research, Pakistan. In this book, Osama describes the situation of Muslims around the world who are humiliated and divided by *kafir*s, and encourages them to unite and fight to release Islam and Muslims. See Lambaga Study dan Penelitian Pakistan, *Membangun Kekuatan Islam di tengah Perselisihan Ummat* (Yogyakarta: Wihdah Press, 2001).

REFERENCES

Abdurrahman, Hafidz. 2002. "Men-'Afghanistan-kan' Negeri-Negeri Islam." *Al-Wa'ie* 18, no. 2 (February): 17.

Ahmed, Akbar S. 2003. *Islam under Siege: Living Dangerously in a Post-Honour World*. Oxford: Polity Press.

Aho, James A. 1994. *This Thing of Darkness: A Sociology of the Enemy*. Seattle: University of Washington Press.

Al-Anshari, Fauzan. 2002. *Terorisme dalam Perspektif Barat dan Islam*, Parts 1–4. http:/majelis.mujahidin.or.id

———. 2002. *Saya Teroris? Sebuah Pledoi*. Jakarta: Penerbit Republika.

Al-Amin, Abu Haris. 2003. "Dakwah Islam: Pemikian, Politik, dan Tanpa Kekerasan." Presented in public discussion under the topic "Islam Identik Kekerasan?" Mandala Bhakti Wanitatama. Yogyakarta, September 14.

Al-Chaidar and Tim Peduli tapol International Amnesty. 1998. *Bencana kaum Muslimin di Indonesia 1980–2000*. Yogyakarta: Wihdah Press.

Al-Jawi, Muhammad Shiddiq. 2003. "Fundamentalisme: Tuduhan Yang Tendensius." Article presented in Tashwirul Afkar journal discussion in *IAIN Sunan Kalijaga*. Yogyakarta.

Amhar, Fahmi. 2003. "Menyambut Perang Salib Baru." *Al-Wa'ie* 3, no. 31 (March).

Arberry, A. J. 1996. *The Koran Interpreted*. New York: Simon and Schuster.

Asy-Syawakili, Muhammad. 2001. "Reposisi Makna Jihad." *Al-Wa'ie* 2, no. 15 (November): 33.

Azzam, Abdullah. *Wasiat Asy-Syahid*. http://www.majelis.mujahidin.or.id.

Awwas, Irfan S. 2003a. *Menelusuri Jejak Jihad S.M. Kartosuwiryo*. Yogyakarta: Wihdah Press.

———. 2003b. *Dakwah dan Jihad Abu Bakar Ba'asyir*. Yogyakarta: Wihdah Press.

———, ed. 2003c. "*Kembali Pada Keyakinan Agama, Forum refleksi kelompok Antar Iman Se-Indonesia.*" Topic of the forum was "*Agama dan Kekerasan: Perspektif Historis-Teologis Karangasem.*" Bali, February 19.

Ba'asyir, Abu Bakar. 2003. Pidato *Amanah Amirul Mujahidin*. Read in Second Mujahidin Congress, Solo.

———. n.d. *Mengenal Watak Orang Kaafir*. Cassette. Surakarta: Al-Ghuraba Records.

Bashari, Luthfi. 2002. *Musuh Besar Umat Islam: Zioneisme, Sekularisme, Atheisme, Sinkretisme, Salibisme, JIL dan Oportunisme.* Yogyakarta: Wihdah Press.

Burhanuddin. 2000. "Syari'at Islam: Pandangan Muslim Liberal." http://www.Islamlib.com, 20/7/2003.

Chua, Amy. 2003. *World on Fire: How Exporting Free Market Democracy Breeds Ethnic Hatred and Global Instability.* New York: Doubleday.

Economist. 2003. "George's Big Adventure." November 29.

Effendi, Bahtiar. 2003. *Islam and the State in Indonesia.* Singapore: Institute of Southeast Asian Studies.

El Fadl, Khalid Abou. 2002. "The Orphan of Modernity in the Clash of Civilizations." *Global Dialogue* 4, no. 2 (Spring).

Erickson, Marc. 2000. "The Osama bin Laden and al-Qaeda of Southeast Asia." *Asia Times.* http://www.atimes.com/se-asia/.

Esack, Farid. 1999. "Muslims Engaging the Other and the Humanum." In *Proselytization and Communal Self-Determination in Africa,* ed. Abdullahi Ahmad An-Naim. Maryknoll, NY: Orbis Books.

——. 1997. *Qur'an, Liberation and Pluralism: An Islamic Perspective of Interreligious Solidarity against Oppression.* Oxford: Oneworld.

Esposito, John L. 2002. *Unholy War: Terror in The Name of Islam.* New York: Oxford University Press.

Galfarsoro, Imanol. "Symbolic Violence and Linguistic Habitus." In *Pierre Bourdieu: An Instance of the Language is Power.* http://www.ibslgu.ac.uk/forum/bourdieu/.

Hizbut Tahrir. n.d.a. "Agar Memerangi Korupsi Tak Sebatas Jargon." *Al-Islam* 10 (182).

——. n.d.b. "Amerika Harus Dilawan!" *Al-Islam* 10 (140): 2.

——. n.d.c. "Barat Menebar Teror di Dunia Islam." *Al-Islam* 8 (94).

——. n.d.d. "Benturan Peradaban Dibalik Serbuan AS." *Al-Islam* 8 (182): 2–3.

——. n.d.e. "Berfikir dalam Konteks Politik." *Al-Islam* 10 (168).

——. n.d.f. "Dibalik Jerat Hutang IMF." *Al-Islam* 5 (100).

——. n.d.g. "Harga Mahal Demokras." *Al Islam* 7 (43).

——. n.d.h. "Invasi Ke Irak: Perang Ideologis." *Al-Islam* 10 (149).

——. n.d.i. "Islam Memberi Rahmat Bagi Semua." *Al-Islam* 8 (185).

———. n.d.j. "Menyambut Idul Adhha 1423 H: Mengembalikan Kemulyaan Umat Islam." *Al-Islam* 10 (141): 1.

———. n.d.k. "Muslim Uzbek: Korban Terrorisme Karimov dan AS." *Al-Islam* 9 (114).

———. n.d.l. "Syari'at Islam: Pilihan Akal Sehat." *Al-Islam* 9 (102).

———.n.d.m. "Waspadai Intervensi Asing dalam Kasus Aceh." *Al-Islam* 10 (155).

———. n.d.n. *The Conflict Between the Democratic System and the Ruling System in Islam.* http://www.khilafah.org/phase1/khilafah/islam/.

———. 1996. *The American Campaign to Suppress Islam.* London: Hizbut Tahrir Publications.

———. 1999a. *The Methodology of Hizbut-Tahrir for Change.* London: Al-Khilafah Publications.

———. 1999b. *Peradaban Barat.* Translated into Indonesian by Muhammad Shiddiq Al-Jawi. London: Hizbut Tahrir Publications.

———. 1999c. *Persepsi-Persepsi Berbahaya Untuk MengantamIislam dan Mnegokohkan.*

———. 2000a. "Antara Yahudi dan Amerika: Siapa Mendominasi Siapa?" *Al-Wa'ie* 1, no. 3 (November): 7–13.

———. 2000b. *The Inevitability of the Clash of Civilizations.* London: Al-Khilafah Publications.

———. 2000c. "Pluralism." *Al-Wa'ie* 1, no. 1 (September): 16.

———. 2000d. "Punahnya Bangsa Yahudi." *Al-Wa'ie* 1, no. 4 (December): 5.

———. 2001a. "Al-Qur'an dan As-Sunnah." *Al-Wa'ie* 2, no. 19 (March): 35–36.

———. 2001b. "Amerika: Teroris Berwajah Manis." *Al-Wa'ie* 1 (7): 27–29.

———. 2001c. "Dialog Antar Agama: Bahaya Terselubung." *Al-Wa'ie* 1, no. 5 (December): 22.

———. 2001d. "Dilema Penerapan Syari'at Islam di Negara Sekuler." *Al-Wa'ie* 1, no. 11 (July): 7.

———. 2001e. "Maluku, Perang Salib dari Masa ke Masa." *Al-Wa'ie* 1, no. 12 (August): 24–28.

———. 2001f. "Melurskan Makna Jihad." *Al-Wa'ie* 6, no. 9 (May): 22.

———. 2001g. "Penghianatan Terhadap Kashmir." Leaflet, Hizabut Tahrir Pakistan, July 13.

———. 2001h. "Revitalisasi Ideologi Islam: Langkah Prakatis Menghadang Laju Imperialism." *Al-Wa'ie* 6, no. 12 (August): 14–17.

———. 2001i. "Revitalisasi Negara Islam." *Al-Wa'ie* 2, no. 15 (November): 17.

———. 2001j. "Seorang Penulis AS Menyerukan untuk Menghancurkan Ka'bah." *Al-Wa'ie* 2, no. 15 (November): 25.

———. 2001k. "Terorisme: Stempel AS Bagi Musuh-Musuhnya." *Al-Wa'ie* 1, no. 7 (March): 7.

———. 2002a. "Agenda Imperialisme Barat." *Al-Wa'ie* 3 (29): 36.

———. 2002b. "Aljazair Dan Wajah Buruk Demokrasi." *Al-Wa'ie* 3, no. 28 (December): 55–59.

———. 2002c. "Isyarat Kegagalan Makar Kaafir Barat." *Al-Wa'ie* 2, no. 17 (January): 3–4.

———. 2002d. "Kashmir Menderita Di Bawah India." *Al-Wa'ie* 2, no. 18 (February): 43–47.

———. 2002e. "Kemenangan Islam dan Kembalinya Khilafah Islamiyah Menurut Isyarat Al-Qur'an dan As-Sunnah." *Al-Wa'ie* 2, no. 19 (March): 5–36.

———. 2002f. "Turkestan Timur Bertahan Di Balik Tirai Bambu." *Al-Wa'ie* 2, no. 23 (July): 43–46.

———. 2003a. "Agenda Imperialisme Barat." *Al-Wa'ie* 3 (29): 36.

———. 2003b. "Antara Imperialisme dan Futuhat." *Al-Wai'ie* 3, no. 31 (March): 3–4.

———. 2003c. "HT Non-Kekerasan." *Al-Wa'ie* 3, no. 35 (July): 31.

Iskandar, Arif B. 2001. "Nasionalisme dan Disintegrasi Umat Islam." *Al-Waie* 1, no. 8 (April): 14–16.

———. 2002. "Revisi dan Reposisi Partai Islam." *Al-Wa'ie* 2, no. 22 (June): 8–9.

Ismail, Abu. 2003. "Di Balik Perang Salib Baru." *Al-Wa'ie* 3, no. 31 (March): 9.

Jati, Sigit Purnawan. 2002. "Jihad Bukan Kejahatan!" *Al-Waie* 2, no. 28 (December): 34–35.

Jaya, Tun Kelana. 2002. "Dibalik Ambruknya Sistem Keuangan Global." *Al-Wa'ie* 3, no. 25 (September): 7–12.

Jeurgensmeyer, Mark. 2000. *Terror in the Mind of God: The Global Rise of Religious Violence.* Berkeley: University of California Press.

Jones, Sydney. 2002. "The Case of 'Ngruki Network' in Indonesia." International Crisis Center, August.

Kastor, Rustam. 2000a. "Badai Pembalasan Laskar Mujahidin Ambon dan Maluku." Yogyakarta: Wihdah Press.

———. 2000b. *Kospirasi Politik RMS dan Kristen Menghancurkan Ummat Islam di Maluku dan Ambon.* Yogyakarta: Wihdah Press.

———. 2000c. *Suara Maluku Membantah Rustam Kastor Menjawab.* Yogyakarta: Wihdah Press.

Komisi AD/ART, Kongres Mujahidin Kedua. Personal communication, Solo, September 2003.

Kurnia, MR. 2002. "Menggagas Kerjasama Antar Partai Islam." *Al-Wa'ie* 2, no. 22 (June).

Liddle, William. 1998. "Skripturalism Miedia Dakwah: Suatu Bentuk pemikiran dan aksi Politik Islam di Indonesia Masa Orde Baru." In *Jalan Baru Islam: Memetakan Paradigma Mutakhir Islam Indonesia,* ed. Mark. R. Woodward. Bandung: Mizan Press.

Maman, Kh. 2001. "Mengakhiri Hukum Positif." *Al-Wa'ie* 2 (16): 7–13.

Mengenal Majelis Mujahidin. "Markaz Pusat Majelis Mujahidin, Jl." Veteran No. 17 Yogyakarta, 19.

MMI. n.d.a. *Usulan Amandemen UUD '45.*

———. n.d.b. *Usulan Undang-Undang Hukum Pidana Republik Indonesia Disesuaikan dengan Syari'at Islam.* Yogyakarta: Markaz Pusat Majelis Mujahidin.

Mujani, Saiful and R. William Liddle. 2004. "Islamism in Democratic Indonesia: Finding of a New Survey." *Journal of Democracy,* January.

Pocket World in Figures, 2003 Edition. 2002. London: *The Economist,* in association with Profile Books, Ltd.

Prasetyo, Eko. 2002. *Membela Agama Tuhan: Potret Gerakan Islam dalam Pusaran Konflik Global.* Yogyakarta: Insist Press.

Purwandana, Adi. 2002. "Perlawanan Total untruk Israel dan Sekutunya." *Al-Wa'ie* 2, no. 22 (June): 5.

Ramadlan, SF, Syamsuddin. 2002. "Khilafah Islamiyah: Keniscayaan Sejarah." *Al-Wa'ie* 2 (19): 12.

Romli, Syamsul M., Asep. 2000. *Demonologi Islam: Upaya Barat Membasmi Kekuatan Islam.* Jakarta: Gema Insani Press.

Sabili. 1999. Vol. 4, no. 20 (April 21).

———. 2003. Vol. 10, no. 24 (April 24).

Sajid, Ahmad. 2001a. "Benturan Peradaban: keniscayaan Sejarah." *Al-Wa'ie* 2, no. 15 (November): 10.

———. 2001b. "Demokrasi: Peradaban Sampah." *Al-Wa'ie* 2, no. 14 (October): 30–35.

Sajidah, Najmah and Khusnul Khatimah. 2001. "Arus Balik Feminism." *Al-Wa'ie* 2, no. 16 (December): 34–37.

Shalih, Sa'aduddin As-Sayyid. 1999. *Jaringan Konspirasi Menentang Islam*. Trans. Muhammad Thalib. Yogyakarta: Wihdah Press.

Salim, Fathi. 2003. "Perang Peradaban." *Al-Wa'ie*, no. 34 (June): 42.

Salmi, Jamil. 2003. *Kekerasan dan Kapitalisme: Pendekatan Baru dalam Melihat Hak-Hak Asasi Manusia*. Trans. Agung Prihantoro. Yogyakarta: Pustaka Pelajar and Komite Untuk Anti Kekerasan (KUAK).

Sukirno, Bambang. "Makar Ahlul Kitab Dalam Lintasan Sejarah." http://www.al-islam.or.id.

Tanjung, Ihsan. "Invasi AS Akan Menyinghkap Semua Ini." *Sabili*, 20.

Tempo. 2003a. October 12: 144.

———. 2003b. October 26: 145.

Thahan, Mahmud. 2001. "Modernisasi Agama: Membunuh Karakter Agama (Satu Dasawarsa Gagasan Pembeharuan Hasan at-Turabi)." *Al-Wa'ie* 2, no. 14 (October): 27–28.

Thalib, Muhammad and Irfan S. Awwas, eds. 1999. *Doktrin Zionisme dan Ideologi Pancasila: Menguak Tabir Pemikiran Politik Founding Fathers RI*. Yogyakarta: Wihdah Press.

Tibi, Bassam. 1998. *The Challenge of Fundamentalism: Political Islam and the New World Disorder*. Berkeley: University of California Press.

Yunanto, S. et al. 2003. *Militant Islamic Movements in Indonesia and Southeast Asia*. Jakarta: Friederich Ebert Stiftung and the Ridep Institute.

Zada, Khamami. 2002. *Islam Radikal: Pergulatan Ormas-Ormas Islam Garis Keras di Indonesia*. Jakarta: Teraju.

Zallum, Abdul Qodim. 2001. *Demokrasi Sistem Kufur: Haram Mengambilnya, Menerapkannya dan Menyebarluaskannya*. Trans. Muhammad Shiddiq al-Jawi. Bandung: Pustaka Thoriqul 'Izzah.

Lightning Source UK Ltd.
Milton Keynes UK
UKHW010354090121
376694UK00004B/175